NATURAL HISTORY
of the
BLACK HILLS AND BADLANDS

Sven G. Froiland

Dr. Sven G. Froiland is Emeritus Professor of Biology and Emeritus Director of the Center for Western Studies of Augustana College, Sioux Falls, South Dakota.

He received his Ph.D. degree in biology from the University of Colorado, Boulder. He was awarded an honorary doctorate of Humanities degree from Luther College, Decorah, Iowa in 1976. A member of numerous professional biological and historical organizations and societies, he is a past president of The South Dakota Academy of Science. He was elected to the South Dakota Heritage Hall of Fame in 1987.

Early in his career he served as a research associate with the Forest Service in the Black Hills. It was at this time that he became fascinated with the complexity of the Hills and has been a serious student of this magnificent area ever since.

Ronald R. Weedon

Dr. Ronald R. Weedon is Professor of Biology and Director of the Chadron State College Herbarium (with its Claude A. Barr and Dr. George R. Morgan Memorial Archives). A faculty member at Chadron State since 1971, Dr. Weedon received his Bachelor of Science degree in Biology from the College of Idaho in Caldwell. The work toward his M.A. and Ph.D. degrees in Botany was done at the University of Kansas, Lawrence. An author of more than sixty scientific papers, Dr. Weedon works with both undergraduate and graduate students on research devoted to the Botany and Ecology of the Great Plains and Black Hills. He is a member of the Board of Directors of the Mammoth Site in Hot Springs and the Chadron State College Research Institute.

NATURAL HISTORY
of the
BLACK HILLS AND BADLANDS

by

SVEN G. FROILAND

Emeritus Professor of Biology
and
Emeritus Director, The Center for Western Studies
Augustana College

BADLANDS

by

RONALD R. WEEDON

Professor of Biology
and
Director of the Herbarium
Chadron State College

THE CENTER FOR WESTERN STUDIES
Augustana College
Sioux Falls, South Dakota
1999

Cover design by Fenske Printing, Inc.
Cover photography courtesy of SD Tourism
 and Badlands Natural History Association

Library of Congress Cataloging-in-Publication Data

Froiland, Sven G.
  Natural history of the Black Hills and Badlands.

  "Part V: Badlands by Ronald R. Weedon."
  Includes bibliographical references.
  1. Natural history—South Dakota—Badlands
National Park. 2. Natural history—Black Hills
(S.D. and Wyo.)
I. Weedon, Ronald R., 1939-   . II. Title.
QH105.S8F76 1990   508.783'9   90-1996
ISBN 0-931170-46-X
ISBN 0-931170-47-8 (pbk.)

PREFACE

There are a great many interesting and colorful publications relating to the Black Hills. Among them are factual scientific and historical volumes, special interest works, and much fiction and folklore. Almost without exception, each covers a single aspect of information that is either very specific and detailed or very general. Thus there is a definite need for a broad natural history of this area which brings together in one publication information from many disciplines all relating to this delightful and fascinating segment of our "land of infinite variety." This volume is an attempt to present selected information about the Black Hills that is of more than ordinary interest to the naturalist, scholar, or vacationer.

The book is divided into three parts, each with a different emphasis and appeal to persons with varying experience and interests. The first part includes information of a general geological nature; the second is historical and includes a lengthy section on South Dakota Indians; the third contains selected material of a biological nature. The design is such that each of the three parts can be read as a separate section. There has been no attempt made to unify the three, either as to style or content. It should be understood that there was no intention to present a complete, detailed treatise of each respective discipline; rather, each section is intended as an overview of, or introduction to, what can be found here with the objective of providing some aid in understanding what the Hills are today and what they once were. Obviously any portion could have been covered in more detail and additional topics might have been included. However, it was necessary to be selective . . . therefore those topics of most interest to most people were included. A fourth part (a series of appendices) has been added, including additional information on related topics not included in the text. This part provides the reader who desires additional information a ready reference to this material. The information contained, coming from many disciplines, has only one common theme . . . the Black Hills.

PREFACE TO THE REVISED EDITION

This edition, with minor changes, purposefully retains the basic material of the original book. The major changes are: (1) a section has been included on *The Current Environment of the Hills* with some observations on the current status of selected wildlife species. This section was added because of the concerns that I, and countless others, share in regard to the environmental changes that have occurred, and continue to occur, in the time that has lapsed since the publication of the first edition, a little more than a decade ago, and, (2) The addition of a section on the *Badlands,* written by Dr. Ronald Weedon of Chadron State College. This section also includes material on the Hot Springs Mammoth Site. This was a natural addition for several reasons including the Badlands' proximity to the Black Hills, their uniqueness in a different way from the uniqueness of the Hills, and their own geological, biological and historical importance.

The basic material presented in the first edition was retained in order to give the reader a proper background and perspective of what the Hills represent and to establish a comparative basis for the proper understanding of how rapidly changes in a natural area can occur. It, hopefully, also may be of help in understanding the current pressures that are being exerted on the Hills' environment by the forces of change.

Sven G. Froiland

The Limestone Bluffs
Custer, South Dakota
1990

ACKNOWLEDGMENTS

I wish to express my personal thanks to the many people who have aided in the preparation of the revised edition of this book, particularly those who offered suggestions and provided current information. I am especially indebted to Dr. Ron Weedon for his section on the Badlands, and to Dave Strain and Arkie Snocker for their persistent encouragement to publish this revision.

I wish to thank David Ode, Ted Benzon, Les Rice, Blair Waite, and Gary Marrone, professional biologists of the South Dakota Department of Game, Fish and Parks, for their valuable contributions on the current status of the flora and fauna of the Hills; and a special thank you to Les Baylor, for his suggestions on the current status of the birds of the area.

I also would like to acknowledge the assistance of the current staff of the Center for Western Studies, Arthur Huseboe, Dean Schueler, Harry Thompson, and especially Barbara Ries.

Finally, I wish to again express my thanks and gratitude to my wife, Marion, for her perpetual patience, encouragement, and understanding.

TABLE OF CONTENTS

List of Illustrations

This photo of the Black Hills, a Mosaic of Landsat images, taken from an altitude in excess of 500 miles, is a "false color" image. The red tones are living vegetation, the blues are sparse vegetation and barren soils, the light tones, are stubble fields.

Photo courtesy of NASA and EROS DATA CENTER,
Sioux Falls, South Dakota

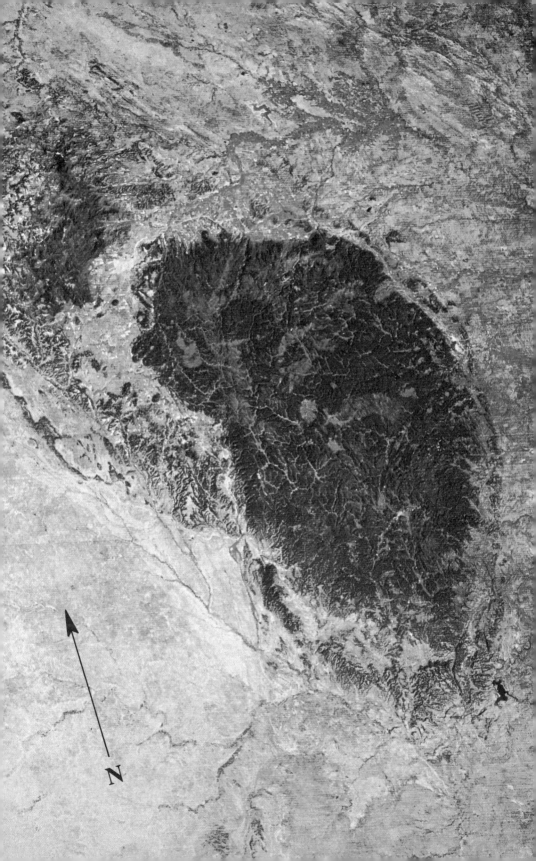

N

INTRODUCTION

"A forested island in a grassland sea" is a descriptive phrase that graphically portrays the Black Hills. To the uninitiated, the term *hills* may be misleading for it is a mountainous upthrust, a tranquil natural area of pine and spruce-covered mountains and hills, canyons and gulches, interspersed with fertile valleys and natural parks or upland prairies, through which flow clear streams. All of these combine to make the Black Hills a lush, green outpost isolated in the center of the relatively vast semi-arid, undulating, high Plains. The Lakota, or Teton Sioux, as well as other Indians, identified this beautiful mountainous area by the name Paha Sapa...Hills that are Black...the abode of thunders. The French voyageurs described them as the Cotes Noire; the early Spanish explorers identified them as Costa Negra. The designation "black" was apparently taken from the fact that the ponderosa pine forests so characteristic of the Hills appear very dark on the horizon as one approaches them from almost any direction across the miles of high Plains. Historical Indians considered the region as a holy ground, rarely en-croached upon. At least, the assertion is made that the Indians seldom or never lived in the Hills. Although they hunted here, probably because of the abundance and diversity of game, there is no evidence to indicate that they spent much time in the Hills. On the contrary, numerous Indian reports, legends and tradi-tions support the observation that they carefully avoided the area except on special occasions. They kept it more or less as a sanctuary for particular religious or ceremonial rites, or for hunting purposes. This seems well established among the Lakota but whether it was true of their predecessors, the Kiowa and the Cheyenne, is probably less certain. (Recent archeological evidence indicates that earlier man [10,000 to 8,000 yrs. B.C.] probably did frequent or inhabit the Hills. As additional evi-dence is available, this question will be more positively an-swered.) One legend reportedly stated that "the Indians must not

1

live in the Black Hills, for the Great Spirit had reserved the Hills and its glittering treasures as a preliminary resting place for the souls of departed braves, in order that they not be made blind with the splendors of the happy hunting ground when they finally arrived there."* When the Indians did enter the Hills on hunting expeditions, they would frequently hang offerings on the trees or place them on rocks to appease the Thunder Gods they felt were responsible for the mysterious rumblings and shooting fire (lightning) so frequently heard and seen in the Hills. These sometimes terrifying storms certainly must have had a great deal to do with the legends that the Hills were inhabited by powerful gods. Such accounts relate something of the mythology and awe that enshrined the Black Hills in the minds of the early people who knew something of the area.

Lt. Col. R. I. Dodge, a member of the Newton-Jenney Expedition in 1875, writes in his book *The Black Hills,* "Far out of the ordinary lines of plains travel, surrounded on all sides by the arid wastes of the "Bad Lands," by bands of hostile and treacherous savages, the Black Hills loomed up in silent majesty, mysterious, unknown. . . . The Indians, the supposed dwellers in this land, maintained, when questioned about it, the most studied silence, or, even in their most confidential or drunken moments, gave such evasive and unsatisfactory replies as added tenfold to the strength of the mysterious fascination which existed in regard to it. . . . The Black Hills has been to the plains traveler the embodiment of the fullest idea of the mysterious and the unknown."**

To add to the mystery, mountain men and explorers also reported unexplained and mysterious loud noises emerging from the Black Hills. Perhaps the first written account of such things is that reported in Thwaite's edition of the *Journals of Lewis and Clark,* Vol. I, October, 1804. . . . "This M. Jon Vallie (evidently meant for Jean Valle, a fur trapper who Lewis and Clark met in their initial contact with the Cheyenne

---

*Maguire, H. N. 1878. *The Coming Empire.* Sioux City. Reprinted in the Rapid City Daily Journal. February 20, 1926.

**Dodge, Lt. Col. R. I., 1965. *The Black Hills.* Ross & Haines, Minneapolis, Minnesota. 151 pp. Reprint of original, published in 1876.

2

River-Black Hills area) informs us that he wintered last winter (1803) 300 Leagues up the Chien River under the Black mountains, . . . The Black mountains he Says is verry high, and Some parts of it has Snow on it in the Summer great quantities of Pine Grow on the Mountains, a great Noise is heard frequently on those Mountains." There are other accounts of these loud noises (booming noises like the discharge of cannon). There seems to be general agreement that they did not refer to thunder. Apparently there has never been a satisfactory explanation of the noises, but they certainly were impressive enough to have caused early writers and explorers to record them.† It is quite certain that they made an impact not only on the Indians but on the early white men in the region. Watson Parker states: "Other voyageurs also told of the mysterious boomings and bangings, and on the whole endowed the Black Hills with an aura of mystery which would intrigue the curious."*

Colonel Dodge summarizes . . . "The Black Hills country is a true oasis in a wide and dreary desert. The approaches from every direction are through long stretches of inhospitable plains, treeless and broken, in which the supply of water is so saturated with bitter and nauseous alkalies as to be unfit for the continuous use of the white man.

"Nature seems to have been at pains to set barriers around and about it. The barrier plains, cut with innumerable ravines and gorges, the nauseous water, are succeeded on a nearer approach by sharp, steep, almost impassable ridges and cañons, in which scarce any water is to be found.

"Every step towards the heart of these 'sacred fastnesses' is beset with innumerable difficulties. These overcome, the venturous explorer is amply repaid for all his

†*Note:* Hyman Palais in his *Survey of Early Black Hills History, Black Hills Engineer,* Vol. XXVII, No. 1 includes this footnote in regard to the noises. (Undocumented). "These strange rumblings have been attributed to the escape of hydrogen from subterranean beds of burning coal. No visitors to the regions where these noises had been heard fail to mention the curious phenomenon. After the year 1833 the rumblings evidently ceased, for explorers no longer mention hearing them."

*Parker, Watson, 1966. *Gold in the Black Hills.* University of Oklahoma Press, Norman, Oklahoma. 259 pp.

3

hardships and privations. Almost any moderately good country would seem a "Paradise" after passing the "Purgatory" of such approaches to it; but allowing for the full extravagance of pleasure which the traveler must feel under such circumstances, after mature judgement derived from several months of actual sojurn and the cool comparison which a return to civilization enables me to make, I but express my fair and candid opinion when I pronounce the Black Hills, in many respects, the finest country I have ever seen.

"The beauty and variety of the scenery, the excellence of the soil, the magnificence of the climate, the abundance of timber and building-stone, make it a most desirable residence for men who want good homes."*

So it is that through the years . . . nearly a century and a half since white man first discovered them...the Black Hills have held a particular fascination for people. The influence of the Plains Indians and their mythology, the location, resources, such as timber and minerals, and climate of the Black Hills, all have been factors in the development of the area. However, in the end it was probably gold that was primarily responsible for the migration of thousands of people across the Plains to the Hills. Nearly from the beginning of recorded history of the area, gold and rumors of gold played a vital role in driving individual prospectors, eastern business interests and the federal government to the Hills. It is generally conceded that the final opening of the Hills, even in the face of treaties which were to preserve them for the Indians, was to be the result of the pressures of the gold craze. There is ample historical evidence to document this. However, it should be stated that other reasons have been postulated, especially for Custer's interest in the Hills, such as the establishment of a military post, his own interest in personal publicity, and others.** Thus, with such a history, coupled with their scientific uniqueness and natural attractions, it is small wonder that the Black Hills area has developed into an impor-

*Dodge, Lt. Col. R. I. 1965. *The Black Hills.* Ross & Haines, Minneapolis, Minnesota. 151 pp. Reprint of original, published in 1876.

**Krause, Herbert & Gary Olson. 1974. *Prelude to Glory.* Brevet Press, Sioux Falls, South Dakota. 279 pp.

4

tant economic asset, as well as a favorite study, vacation and recreation area.

That the Hills "cast a spell" over those who have spent some time there is nicely described by Leland Case in his Foreword to Jennewein's *Black Hills Book Trails* where he writes: "This book is really a love letter. I know. Anyone would know, if in his boyhood recollections are memories of the ruffled frieze the Black Hills makes along prairie horizons, or if ever he sniffed spruce after a rain in Spearfish Canyon, or if just once he bathed his eyes in the green and buff sweep dropping away from Harney Peak.

"The Sioux and their predecessors lived in fear and awe of the hills, where dwelled their wakan of fire and thunder. Now the fear is gone but the awe lingers—and with it blends an affection that flows between the lines of books people write."*

THE BADLANDS

The Badlands are located southeast of the Black Hills, between the Cheyenne and White rivers. The area is truly a bizarre, primordial, landscape of colorful high table lands, mesas, buttes, precipitous-walled valleys, and myriads of fantastically shaped spires and pinnacles.

Over eons of time the combined forces of water and wind have created a striking topography from the parent sandstone, limestone, shale and clay beds that were deposited as sediment washed from the Black Hills and Rocky Mountain upthrusts. The colors of the geological strata are particularly striking following a rain shower, when the soils are freshly washed.

Now designated the *Badlands National Park,* the area includes over 380 square miles of arid wonderland. Here are one of the world's greatest fossil beds of prehistoric invertebrate and vertebrate animals. During the Oligocene Epoch of the Age of Mammals, beginning approximately 36 million years ago, the area supported incredible numbers of animals such as large sabre-toothed cats,

*Jennewein, J. Leonard. 1962. *Black Hills Book Trails.* Dakota Territory Centennial Commission and Dakota Wesleyan University, Mitchell, South Dakota. 111 pp.

5

miniature horses and camels, oreodonts and titanotheres. For nearly a century individuals, and teams representing many universities, removed countless fossils that are now deposited in major museums. Fortunately, current stringent restrictions prohibit such wholesale collecting, except by special permits exclusively for scientific purposes.

The Badlands were first named *Les Mauvaises Terres a Traverser* (bad lands to travel across) by the early French fur-traders. Native Americans called them the *Mako* (land) *Sica* (bad). Their mystique, uniqueness, and stark exciting beauty, still fascinate people today. One cannot help but feel a strange relationship to the past when standing alone somewhere in these fascinating formations. It is as if one fully expects to see a dinosaur come lumbering over the next butte!

As one stands on a ridge overlooking these "monuments to erosion" their full meaning to all who have been here is difficult to imagine...

> *A place to seek a vision?*
> *A place to avoid?*
> *A paleontologist's dream?*
> *A geologist's field laboratory?*
> *A photographer's paradise?*
> *A wasteland?*
> *A place of natural beauty?*

...whatever, the Badlands deserve much more than an hour's drive through them. They must be experienced to fully appreciate them for what they are.

6

Part I
GENERAL INFORMATION

GEOGRAPHY
TOPOGRAPHY AND GEOLOGY
SOIL
HYDROGRAPHY
GLACIATION
CLIMATE

"During most of the nineteenth century the Black Hills of Dakota were the epitome of the great American dream: The dream of wonders yet untapped, of riches far beyond the rainbow's end, of a great new land of hope and glory, far out beyond the last frontier. Remote, majestic, and unknown, they were guarded alike by distance, treaty, and hostile Indians. The stories which grew up around them, told by the grizzled trapper, subtle half-breed, or chance explorer were those of the dream itself. Here, in the Black Hills, the legends told of wood and water, of open meadows rich with grass and berries, of hills alive with game, of glowing gold in the mountain streams, and of safety from the hostile but fearful Indian tribes. Here indeed was the dream come true; here was the goal of the western movement, here the land of hearts desire.

The Black Hills were indeed the stuff of which great dreams are made. Their rich and fertile valleys, abundant game, and mineral wealth excited all who visited them or heard the garbled tales of Indians and mountain men. By all accounts, they were an earthly paradise beyond the far frontier, the epitome of the American dream."

Taken from, and published with permission of, Watson Parker, 1962. *The Exploration of the Dakota Black Hills.* Unpublished Master's Thesis, University of Oklahoma, Norman.

9

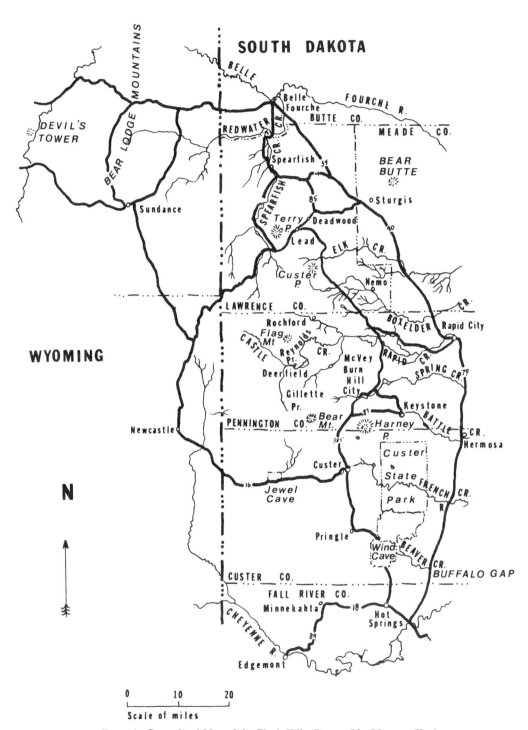

Figure 1. Generalized Map of the Black Hills. Prepared by Maureen Kaul.

10

GEOGRAPHY

The Black Hills are an isolated, unglaciated, and distinctive group of mountains that rise high above the surrounding Plains on the west-central border of South Dakota. As the easternmost extension of the Rocky Mountains, the uplift covers an elliptical area of nearly 6,000 square miles, extending approximately 120 miles in a north-south direction and approximately 40-50 miles in an east-west direction. Although the greater bulk of the uplift is situated in South Dakota, a much smaller segment, the Bear Lodge Mountains, extends to the northwest a short distance into the northeast corner of Wyoming (Fig. 1). The Bighorn Mountains to the west and the Laramie Mountains to the southwest at a distance of approximately 150 to 200 miles are the nearest mountain ranges. There are many formational similarities between the Black Hills and the Bighorn Mountains, especially. The Black Hills are essentially a dome structure, sloping more steeply to the east than to the west, rising 3,000 to 4,000 feet above the surrounding northern Great Plains. The highest point, Harney Peak, has an elevation of 7,242 feet. In the surrounding Plains, elevations range from approximately 3,000 to 3,500 feet on the northern, eastern and southern edges of the uplift. On the western edge, the elevations are higher, averaging about 4,500 feet.

TOPOGRAPHY AND GEOLOGY

The major topographical features, as identified and well described by Darton and Paige in their *Description of the Central Black Hills,** are: the Hogback Ridge, the Red Valley, the Limestone Plateau, and the Central Area, which includes the Harney Range (Fig. 2).

The Hogback Ridge forms the actual outer rim of the Black Hills, encircling the uplift proper. The Hogback is a more or less

---

*Darton, N. H., and Sidney Paige, 1925. *Central Black Hills Folio.* U.S. Geol. Surv. Bull. 219, 34 pp.

11

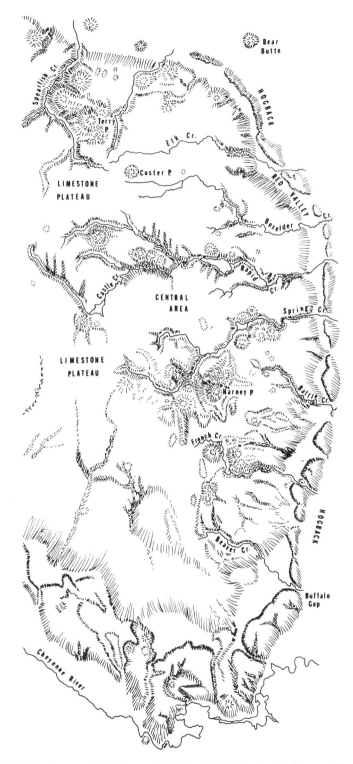

Figure 2. Major Topographic Features of the Black Hills. Drawing by Maureen Kaul.

12

single hard sandstone ridge rising out of the plains as the initial foothills formation. The outer slope presents a more or less gradual incline from the plains to the crest, whereas the inner slope is typically more abrupt facing the Red Valley. The altitude of the ridge varies from approximately 3,800 feet in the Rapid City area to 4,900 feet in the Elk Mountain area in the southwest. The major streams flowing out from the Hills have eroded gaps in the ridge representing the only breaks in a nearly continuous outer circle. Buffalo Gap, so named because large herds of bison migrated through this gap between the Plains and

Bison grazing in Custer State Park. Photo by author, 1976.

the grasslands of the Red Valley, is perhaps the most well-known of the breaks in the Hogback. The sandstone consists of a coarse gray to green or buff conglomerate interbedded with buff, red, and gray clay toward the top. The major constituent of the ridge is sandstone of the Lakota formation. In addition, other elements of the Inyan Kara group are present, including Fall River sandstone, Fuson shale and Minnewasta limestone, all of the Lower Cretaceous Period. The ridge is invariably covered with Ponderosa pine. Toward the upper portions of the ridge one can expect to find petrified wood.

13

Classic Relief Map of the Black Hills. Originally prepared for the World's Fair Commission in 1904. Reproduced in several publications.

14

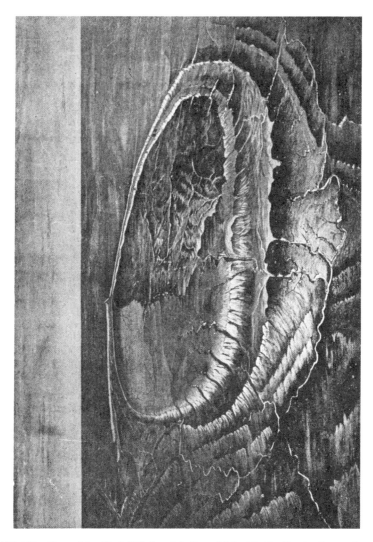

NORTH

"Bird Eye View of the Black Hills", originally published in the Newton-Jenney Survey Report of 1875. This photo has been reproduced in numerous publications on the Black Hills.

15

The outer slope, generally devoid of trees, consists of limestone of the Greenhorn formation covered by several hundred to several thousand feet of shales deposited by very muddy seas during the Upper Cretaceous Period. These shales, the most obvious being the Pierre shale, contain abundant fossils. The Pierre shale forms one of the major constituents of the soil of the "west river country" of the state. The Pierre shale area is sometimes called the "gumbo region" because of the plastic clay which weathers from the shale.

The Red Valley or "racetrack", situated immediately inside of the Hogback Ridge, is also almost continuous and encircles the Black Hills. The valley ranges in width from a narrow band to several miles at its widest point, and in altitude from approximately 3,300 feet to 3,500 feet. The soil is red and consists of sandstones, sandy clay, and shales of the Sundance and Spearfish formations of the Triassic and Jurassic Periods. The Red Valley does not support a well-developed vegetation; in fact, there is an almost total absence of trees here, probably due to the generally dry conditions and high concentrations of salts in the soil.

The Limestone Plateau is a high, relatively flat escarpment located inward from the Red Valley, attaining its greatest breadth along the northwestern edge of the Black Hills, from the Spearfish canyon area west to the Wyoming line. It extends from approximately 2 miles to 15 miles across, with the widest part in the west. The plateau forms the main divide of the Hills and attains an elevation of 7,100 feet at the highest point. Comprised of Paleozoic sediments, it consists of limestone of the Englewood formation, Devonian Period, displaying a pink to buff color; and Pahasapa (Madison) of the Mississipian Period, a massive light-colored formation. In addition sandstones and dolomite shales of the Deadwood, Whitewood, and Minnelusa formations occur.

One of the distinctive features characteristic of the plateau is the occurrence of high spectacular cliffs projecting above the valley floor. Extensive pine and spruce forests occur throughout the area. The soil is fertile, but water is usually limited due to the porosity of the rocks. The vast majority of the caves in the Hills occur in the Limestone.

16

The last of the four features described by Darton is the Central Area, forming the main core or central mass of the Black Hills from which all sedimentary formations have been eroded. This area includes the Harney Range and consists of highly dissected ridges and mountains scattered among large valleys, with canyons extending out of a considerable variety of Pre-Cambrian igneous and sedimentary rocks (schists, slates, quartzites) in different stages of metamorphosis, together with granite and pegmatite. The most rugged portion of the Hills, this area is represented by numerous highly eroded pinnacles, knobs, and mountains. Perhaps special attention should be directed to the great masses of granite which occur in this area. Granite

The Needles Formation, Custer State Park. Photo by author, 1976.

weathers much less readily than its accompanying materials; thus it forms the major topographic features of the Central area. The altitude of the Central Area varies from approximately 5,000 to 6,000 feet for the most part, with several prominent up-thrusts: the famous Harney Peak (7,242 feet) and the Needles formation; Bear Mountain, southwest of Hill City (7,166 feet); Terry Peak, west of Lead (7,071 feet); Custer Peak, south of

17

Lead-Deadwood (6,794 feet). The soils of the Central Area are thin and coarse at higher elevations, the result of the slow breakdown of quartz and the large crystals in the granites. At lower elevations and in the valleys the soil is more of a sandy loam.

The Harney Range. Photo courtesy Robert Evenson, 1977.

In addition to the four major features described by Darton, a fifth element might be included, namely the Foothills and Minnekahta Plains. This area is situated between the Red Valley and the Limestone Plateau. In the southern Hills it consists of a broad rolling tableland, the Minnekahta Plains. In the northern and eastern Black Hills it is a narrower, more typical foothills area, marking the transition from plains to mountainous topography. The soil is derived from slabby red sandstones, shales, and limestone (see note below.)

Outside the Hills proper there are two geologically significant and interesting formations: (1) Bear Butte, an igneous isolated dome, 4,422 feet, located just east of Sturgis, and (2) Devil's Tower, rising to an altitude of 5,117 feet on the western edge of the Bear Lodge Mountains in Wyoming.

Note: for more detailed information on geological formations see p. 24, Fig. 3, General Outcrop Section of the Black Hills Area.

18

Minnekahta Plains. Photo by author, 1976.

GEOLOGIC HISTORY

The Black Hills, constituting one of the very old regions of the North American continent, have a long and complex history. Although they apparently are not the most ancient lands known (the highly disturbed metamorphics of the Hudson Bay area are commonly recognized as the foundation rocks of the continent), the foundation rocks of the Hills greatly outdate the profound sedimentary series of which the Americas are primarily formed. It should be understood that any adequate discussion of the geologic history of the Hills implies some knowledge of mountain building, a reasonable understanding of a large surrounding area, and true comprehension of geologic time.

Fortunately the exposures of the many rock formations of the Black Hills are abundant and quite generally distributed. These

19

exposures reveal an unusually complete record of the changes that occurred as the region developed. The Black Hills, indeed, represent a classic example of mountain formation by "updoming." As the dome was pushed up, ultimately the top layers were eroded with the result that a "layer cake" effect was produced. As one travels from the outer portions inward, a complete sequence of rock strata is encountered from the more recent formations on the periphery to the oldest in the center. This fact, plus such factors as their age, complexity and the relative ease with which different formations can be located (sections can be found which reveal a continuous age stratification that are easily accessible) has meant that the area is of great geological significance and interest. Thus it has been extensively studied by geologists for nearly a century.

Darton describes the uplift as follows: "It was formed in a wide expanse of almost horizontal beds, the uplift of which has brought above the general level of the plains a mass of Algonkian shists, conglomerate, quartzites, limestones, granites, and associated rocks, around which there is upturned a nearly complete sequence of sedimentary formations ranging in age from Upper Cambrian to latest Cretaceous, all dipping away from the central core. The structure along the sides of the uplift is that of a monocline dipping toward the plains. The oldest Paleozoic beds form an escarpment that faces the central area of crystalline rocks, and each bed passes beneath a younger one in regular succession outward toward the margin of the uplift. The Paleozoic and Mesozoic sedimentary formations consist of a series of thick sheets of sandstones, limestones, and shales, all essentially conformable in attitude. The stratigraphy is in general similar to that of the Rocky Mountains in Colorado and Wyoming but shows many local features."*

The fact that the Black Hills had an ancient beginning is substantiated in that they correspond in age to the oldest mountains on the continent. Two positive age dates document this: (1) a granite-gneiss record from samples taken along Little Elk Creek, approximately 3 miles north of Nemo, Lawrence County,

---

*Darton, N. H., and Sidney Paige, 1925. *Central Black Hills Folio.* U.S. Geol. Surv. Bull. 219, 34 pp.

The Needles Formation. Photo courtesy of Kent Fish, 1971.

21

South Dakota, s ½ sec 3, T3N, R5E. This is along the northeast periphery of the Precambrian core of the Black Hills. Three samples of the total-rock gneiss were analyzed for rubidium and strontium in an effort to determine its age of emplacement. They indicated an age of approximately 2.5 billion years B.P. This work was done by R. E. Zartman, J. J. Norton and T. W. Stern in 1964.* (2) Pegmatites of the Harney peak region have been dated at 1.6 billion years by W. R. Eckelman and J. L. Kulp.** In addition gold isotopes from the Lead area (Homestake mine) have been dated as Pre-Cambrian.

In Pre-Cambrian times the area was covered by a vast inland sea, with heavy deposits of sediments accumulating at the bottom over long periods of geological time. This great deposit of sediments slowly sank under its own weight and ultimately masses of magma surged upward underneath it in response to pressure. The overlying rock was bent into deep folds and much of it was metamorphosed, by heat and pressure, into different kinds of rock. These rocks were then uplifted as the primordial Black Hills. However, by the Cambrian Period erosive forces had worn down these first formed hills to a nearly level surface.

The Pre-Cambrian geology of the Black Hills is summarized as follows in *The Geologic History of the Black Hills* by J. P. Gries and E. L. Tullis, "The pre-Cambrian sedimentary rocks were shale, sandstone, conglomerates, limestones and other carbonate rocks. . . . Sills of diorite and gabbro were intruded toward the close of pre-Cambrian folding and were metamorphosed to amphibolities. Dynamothermal metamorphism changed the sedimentary rocks to schist, slate, quartzite, graywacke and marble. A series of large folds, commonly nearly isoclinal, were formed and superposed on these were minor folds of several orders of magnitude down to microscopic size. The dips commonly are to the east and the plunges of the folds are gentle to almost vertical. . . . The folded rocks were invaded by pre-Cambrian granite now exposed at many places in the

*Zartman, R. E., J. J. Norton & T. W. Stern. 1964. *Ancient Granite-Gneiss in the Black Hills, South Dakota.* Science, Vol. 145, No. 3631, pp. 479-481.

**Eckleman, W. R. and J. L. Kulp. 1957. *Uranium—Lead Method of Age Determination.* Part II: North American Localities. Bull. Geol. Soc. Amer. Vol. 68, pp. 1117-1140.

22

southern Black Hills, including Harney Peak and Mt. Rushmore. The granite extends to the southeast beneath the Paleozoic cover. In the northern Black Hills there were scattered areas of pre-Cambrian granite at Little Elk Creek, Whitewood Peak, Tinton and the Warren Peaks in Bear Lodge Mountains. . . . The later Harney Peak granite consists mostly of microlineperthite, orthoclase, quartz, sodic plagioclase, muscovite and tourmaline. In part it is pegmatitic and is accomplished by a host of pegmatitic intrusions. The pegmatities have made the Black Hills an important or principal producer of feldspar, mica, lithium minerals, beryl, columbite-tantalite and other rare minerals. The pre-Cambrian granite also brought minor deposits of gold, silver, lead, zinc, and tungsten."*

Over the extensively long period of time between the Cambrian and the Tertiary Periods (from approximately 600 million to 60 million years B.P.), evidence indicates that there were tremendous forces at work causing intermittent domal uplifts alternating with extensive erosion cycles and lengthy periods of advancing seas alternating with receding seas covering a large area surrounding what was to become the Black Hills. There were major seas during each of the geologic Periods, individually producing new layers of sedimentary deposits. Probably toward the end of the Cretaceous Period, the final retreat of the great seas occurred. (For more detailed information on geological formations, see Fig. 3, p. 24, *A General Outcrop Section of the Black Hills Area,* prepared and published by the Department of Geology and Geological Engineering of the South Dakota School of Mines and Technology, Rapid City. The section is included with the kind permission of the Department.)

There were then inaugurated some of the greatest mountain building movements in the history of the continent. . . . The Black Hills uplifted again into an elongated dome, the forerun-

---

*Gries, J. P. and E. L. Tullis. 1955. *The Geologic History of the Black Hills.* Guidebook, Black Hills Field Conference, North Dakota Geologic Society. pp. 31-36. Conrad, Bismark, N. Dakota.

Fig. 3

GENERAL OUTCROP SECTION OF THE BLACK HILLS AREA

	FORMATION		SECTION	THICKNESS IN FEET	DESCRIPTION
QUATERNARY	SANDS AND GRAVELS			0-50	Sand, gravel, and boulders.
TERTIARY — PLIOCENE	OGALLALA GROUP			0-100	Light colored sands and silts.
TERTIARY — MIOCENE	ARIKAREE GROUP			0-500	Light colored clays and silts. White ash bed at base
TERTIARY — OLIGOCENE	WHITE RIVER GROUP			0-600	Light colored clays with sandstone channel fillings and local limestone lenses
TERTIARY — PALEOCENE	FORT UNION FORMATION	TONGUE RIVER MEMBER		0-425	Light colored clays and sands, with coal-bed farther north.
		CANNONBALL MEMBER		0-225	Green marine shales and yellow sandstones, the latter often as concretions.
		LUDLOW MEMBER		0-350	Somber gray clays and sandstones with thin beds of lignite.
?	HELL CREEK FORMATION (Lance Formation)			425	Somber-colored soft brown shale and gray sandstone, with thin lignite lenses in the upper part. Lower half more sandy. Many loglike concretions and thin lenses of iron carbonate.
CRETACEOUS — UPPER	FOX HILLS FORMATION			25-200	Grayish-white to yellow sandstone
	PIERRE SHALE			1200-2000	Principal horizon of limestone lenses giving teepee buttes. Dark-gray shale containing scattered concretions. Widely scattered limestone masses, giving small tepee buttes
		Sharon Springs Mem.			Black fissile shale with concretions
	NIOBRARA FORMATION			100-225	Impure chalk and calcareous shale
CRETACEOUS	CARLILE FORMATION	Turner Sand Zone		400-750	Light-gray shale with numerous large concretions and sandy layers.
		Wall Creek Sands			Dark-gray shale
	GREENHORN FORMATION			(25-30)	Impure slabby limestone. Weathers buff.
	GRANEROS GROUP	BELLE FOURCHE SHALE		(200-350)	Dark-gray calcareous shale, with thin Orman Lake limestone at base. Gray shale with scattered limestone concretions.
				300-550	Clay spur bentonite at base.
CRETACEOUS — LOWER		MOWRY SHALE		150-250	Light-gray siliceous shale. Fish scales and thin layers of bentonite.
		NEWCASTLE SANDSTONE		20-60	Brown to light yellow and white sandstone.
		SKULL CREEK SHALE		170-270	Dark gray to black shale
	INYAN KARA GROUP — LAKOTA FM	FALL RIVER [DAKOTA (?)] ss		10-200	Massive to slabby sandstone.
		Fuson Shale		10-188	Coarse gray to buff cross-bedded conglomeratic ss, interbedded with buff, red, and gray clay, especially toward top. Local fine-grained limestone.
		Minnewaste ls		0-25	
				25-485	
	MORRISON FORMATION			0-220	Green to maroon shale. Thin sandstone.
JURASSIC	UNKPAPA SS			0-225	Massive fine-grained sandstone.
	SUNDANCE FM	Redwater Mem, Lak Member, Hulett Member, Stockade Beaver, Canyon Spr. Mem		250-450	Greenish-gray shale, thin limestone lenses. Glauconitic sandstone; red ss. near middle
	GYPSUM SPRING			0-45	Red siltstone, gypsum, and limestone
TRIASSIC ?	SPEARFISH FORMATION			250-700	Red sandy shale, soft red sandstone and siltstone with gypsum and thin limestone layers.
		Goose Egg Equivalent			Gypsum locally near the base.
PERMIAN	MINNEKAHTA LIMESTONE			30-50	Massive gray, laminated limestone.
	OPECHE FORMATION			50-135	Red shale and sandstone
PENNSYLVANIAN	MINNELUSA FORMATION			350-850	Yellow to red cross-bedded sandstone, limestone, and anhydrite locally at top. Interbedded sandstone, limestone, dolomite, shale, and anhydrite. Red shale with interbedded limestone and sandstone at base.
MISSISSIPPIAN	PAHASAPA (MADISON) LIMESTONE			300-630	Massive light-colored limestone. Dolomite in part. Cavernous in upper part.
DEVONIAN	ENGLEWOOD LIMESTONE			30-60	Pink to buff limestone. Shale locally at base.
ORDOVICIAN	WHITEWOOD (RED RIVER) FORMATION			0-60	Buff dolomite and limestone.
	WINNIPEG FORMATION			0-100	Green shale with siltstone.
CAMBRIAN	DEADWOOD FORMATION			10-400	Massive buff sandstone. Greenish glauconitic shale, flaggy dolomite and flatpebble limestone conglomerate. Sandstone, with conglomerate locally at the base.
PRE-CAMBRIAN	METAMORPHIC and IGNEOUS ROCKS				Schist, slate, quartzite, and arkosic grit. Intruded by diorite, metamorphosed to amphibolite, and by granite and pegmatite.

1963

DEPARTMENT OF GEOLOGY AND GEOLOGICAL ENGINEERING
SOUTH DAKOTA SCHOOL OF MINES AND TECHNOLOGY
RAPID CITY, SOUTH DAKOTA

24

ner of the Laramide revolution which raised the Rocky Mountains. Although the exact time of the beginning of the Laramide uplift is uncertain - - - there are no sediments in the Hills to provide evidence as to the time of beginning of the uplift - - - The Black Hills were lifted sometime between the final stages of the Cretaceous and during Paleocene and Eocene times. The oldest Tertiary formations found in the Hills are from the middle Oligocene indicating that uplift, concurrent dissection, and removal of about 6,500 feet of sediment had been accomplished by that time (approximately 36 million years B.P.). Later Cenozoic history of the Hills is imperfectly known. It is apparent that another uplift with folding and faulting occurred in the Miocene followed by erosion in the Pliocene. A final uplift probably occurred about the beginning of the Pleistocene which left basically the current configuration. Active erosive forces and considerable stream adjustment due to the changing conditions of uplift and tilting of the general surface continued during the Pleistocene. Continued erosion aided possibly by additional uplift have allowed the streams to cut through and considerably below the earlier Pleistocene high level deposits and they are now depositing alluvium along their present courses. This uplift also caused the entrenching of some of the streams around the Black Hills.

The best map available on the Geology of the Black Hills is the *Geologic Map of the Black Hills,* published by the South Dakota Geological Survey, Educational Series Map Five, State of South Dakota. This excellent map is included (see foldout at back of book) through special purchase arrangements and with the permission of Dr. Duncan J. McGregor, State Geologist for the State of South Dakota. It is an invaluable primary source of information on the geology of the Hills area. The author is grateful and pleased to be able to include it as a service to the readers of this book.

SOIL

There are three major soil regions in South Dakota: (1) The Chernozem region basically covers the eastern portion of the state, (2) the central and western portions are the Chestnut region, and (3) the Black Hills are identified as the Gray Wooded soil region. The Gray Wooded region is unique for South Dakota because the soils have largely developed under timber in dry subhumid to humid climate, certainly more humid than that of the surrounding plains.

The soils of the Black Hills are difficult to classify, because of the diversified, rugged topography of the area and the variety of parent rock material present. Therefore, most of the soils are unclassified and are generally stony or rocky, as with any mountainous area. The soils are derived from parent materials which include limestone, sandstone, and local alluvium from igneous and metamorphic rocks. Generally, in the mountainous areas and the limestone plateau the soils consist mostly of rock outcrop, excessively drained, since the topography consists of rocky ridges with steep exposed slopes. Some lithosols occur on upper forested slopes. The intermediate woodlands exhibit Gray Wooded soils, particularly in residuum and local alluvium. The lower grassland slopes are covered with a relatively thin Chernozem. The large park-like prairies in the Central Hills exhibit a shallow soil, primarily rocky loams, with deposits of slates underneath and forming sporadic outcrops. The soils along streamsides are typically deep silt loams of variable depth and weak subsoil development. The red-colored soils of the Red Valley consist primarily of Chestnut soils, whereas the Hogback ridge, typically steepsloped, has a soil covering of shallow calcareous lithosols.

There is no definite, detailed work that has been done specifically on the soils of the Black Hills as such. Most of the information that is available on soils is published by individual County Soil Conservation Service agencies or County Extension Services. The best general (brief) summary and description of soils of the Hills was prepared by Dr. Ronald W. Turner, in consultation with the South Dakota Soils and Water Conservation Service, and published in his scholarly work, *Mammals of the Black Hills of South Dakota and Wyoming,* pp. 24-25.* It is included here through the courtesy of The University of Kansas Miscellaneous Publications.

*Turner, Ronald W., 1974. *Mammals of the Black Hills of South Dakota and Wyoming.* Univ. of Kansas, Mus. of Nat. Hist., Miscellaneous Publication No. 60, Lawrence.

SOIL SUMMARY OF THE BLACK HILLS

Mountainland Association.—occupies the Central Basin mountainous core (1200 square miles) of igneous and sedimentary rock; excessively drained; topography: high rocky ridges, narrow rolling plateaus, deeply entrenched canyons, and park-like mountain valleys; exposed slopes: bare rock; steep slopes: Spearfish and Laporte Lithosols; upper forested slopes: Edloe Gray Wooded Soils; intermediate woodland slopes: Chernozem Soils; lower grassland slopes: Chestnut Soils; along valley and canyon drainages: -Table Mountain Soils (alluvial loams, intermixed with loose stones); land use: recreation, major timber production (ponderosa pine), and grazing.

Limestone Plateau Association.—occupies a high plateau of sedimentary rock (sandstone, limestone and shale) that encircles the Central Basin; well-drained; topography: rolling slopes, broad upland valleys, few rocky ridges, buttes and steep canyons; distribution of major soil types as in the Mountainland Association, differing only in percent coverage due to contrasts in topography; rocky silt loams that occupy ridges may be absent on south-facing slopes where stands of pine are thin or absent; grassland soils of some upland valleys have a water table; land use: recreation, some timber production (ponderosa pine and white spruce), grazing, and farming (oats, legumes and tame grasses).

Slate Prairie Association.—occupies three isolated prairies (Reynolds and Gillette Prairies, and the Bald Hills) comprising about 9000 acres in the Central Basin; well-drained; topography: rolling to steeply rounded slopes; shallow rocky loams underlain by slates, some Table Mountain Soils along upland drainages; no evidence of prior forestation; land use: grazing and farming (oats and vegetables).

Undifferentiated Alluvial Association.—occurs along stream channels of all major valley systems in the Black Hills; well-drained, except for some areas of seepage; topography: fairly level to gently undulating; deep silt loams, with weak subsoil development; land use (highly productive, but limited by cool temperatures and short growing season): grazing and farming (oats, alfalfa and hay).

Foothill Transition Association.—intervenes between the Limestone Plateau and Dakota Hogback; well-drained; topography: complexly dissected foothills with gently rounded to steep slopes, and narrow ridges and valleys; land use: recreation, minor timber production (ponderosa pine), grazing, and dryland and irrigational farming. Due to topographical diversity, this region is divided into several subassociations:

   Laporte-Sandoz-Berthoud Subassociaton.—calcareous soils with limestone outcrops often exposed on the surface; Laporte Lithosols: occur on ridge tops and abrupt slopes; Sandoz Chernozems: occupy intermediate woodland slopes; Berthoud Chestnut Soils: occupy alluvial swales and drainageways on lower grassland slopes.

   Spearfish-Neville Subassociation.—reddish-colored Chestnut Soils under grasslands that occupy a valley-like ("race-track") position between the steeper foothills and Dakota Hogback and overlay a gypsum-like shale substratum; Spearfish Soils: occur on gently rolling

27

slopes; Neville Soils: occupy longer and smoother colluvial and residual slopes.

Sand Hill Regosol Subassociation.—sands and fine sandy loams (presumably of the Valentine series) extend northwestward from the Sand Hills of Nebraska, along the Custer County, South Dakota-Weston County, Wyoming border; occur on gently rolling terrain; exposed rock prominent in some areas.

Dakota Hogback Association.—occupies a steep sandstone ridge that encircles the outer limits of the Black Hills; well-drained; topography: abrupt to sloping, with exposed sandstone outcrops; shallow calcareous Travessila Lithosols; land use: grazing.

The *Pierre Shale Plains Association* occurs just exterior to the Black Hills, consisting of grassland Chestnut Soils with moderately deep firm clays overlaying shales, and is penetrated by the *Vale-Beaverton Alluvial Association* that occupies low terraces and benches adjacent to larger streams that flow out from the Hills. Soils of Southwestern South Dakota, excluding the Black Hills, have the palest tone, are browner in hue, and have less organic matter and total nitrogen than soils of other parts of the state.

HYDROGRAPHY

The Black Hills uplift is drained by many relatively small streams radiating from the divide formed by the western part of the Limestone Plateau. Streamflows are greatest where drainage is toward the north and east. Intermittent streams are common in the south, west, and at lower elevations elsewhere. Many streams disappear underground or lose much of their flow when they cross tilted sedimentary beds near the perimeter of the uplift. Spearfish and Boulder Creeks in the northern Hills, for example, become dry creek beds for some distance before they emerge from the Hills and once again become surface streams. The major streams are, from south to north: Fall River in the Hot Springs area; Beaver Creek flowing through Buffalo Gap; Lame Johnny, French and Grace Coolidge Creeks in Custer State Park; Battle Creek, Spring Creek, and Castle Creek which joins Rapid Creek (flowing through Rapid City) in the central Hills; Boxelder and Elk Creeks in the north central area; Bear Butte and Whitewood Creeks to the northeast. One of the largest and most picturesque streams is Spearfish Creek flowing north through the famous Spearfish Canyon and joining the Redwater River just outside the Hills proper north of Spearfish.

28

A second Beaver Creek, west of Spearfish, also flows north and joins the Redwater. All surface flow drains eventually into either of two rivers which nearly encircle the uplift; to the north and east of the Hills the Belle Fourche, or beautiful fork (of the Cheyenne), and to the south and east the Cheyenne River (originally identified as the south fork of the Cheyenne). These rivers join northeast of the Black Hills and flow eastward as the Cheyenne River to join the Missouri River north of Pierre. Alluvial soils along the Belle Fourche and Cheyenne Rivers are quite sandy with windblown areas similar to the Sandhills of south central South Dakota and Nebraska.

Reports of early explorations of the Black Hills made little or no mention of water and watershed conditions. The first significant documentation appeared in the journals of Colonel R. I. Dodge in 1876.* Dodge referred to "well-watered" conditions and numerous streams and springs. He consistently described the streams as cool, clear and pure . . . Riparian (streamside) vegetation was dense, limiting travel along streams, particularily in deep narrow canyons . . . grass was abundant. He also reported that "cool, pure, and abundant as is the water, there are but two varieties of fish in the Hills proper, the sucker and the dace."

Obviously, there have been many significant changes in water conditions in the one hundred plus years since Dodge first described them. One of the most significant changes is the reduction in stream flow. Most, if not all, streams in primary drainages once exhibited a high, fairly stable stream flow, and the forest cover was much less extensive than it is now. The same streams today are low, many reduced to an intermittent level, and the forests are dense. Natural reproduction, especially by Ponderosa pine, is apparently highly favored in the Hills. Dense stands of young trees are found wherever "space is available." Comparisons of photographs taken in the late 1800's with those taken today of the same area consistently reveal major changes from light to dense forest cover. Forest

---

*Dodge, Lt. Col. R. I. 1965. *The Black Hills.* Ross and Haines, Minneapolis, Minn. (reprint of original, published in 1876)

29

fires are better controlled, and although modern forestry management thinning programs are commonplace, the forests are still dense throughout the Hills, exhibiting a closed canopy for the most part. The result is that moisture is largely prevented from reaching underground water tables because it is intercepted by trees. In addition evaporation and transpiration from dense tree stands draw water from the ground, thus reducing the amount of water available for recharging ground water and for runoff. Therefore, most investigators consider the forests as they now exist to be the largest single factor in loss of stream flow in the Hills. However, other factors also are involved: (1) The large increase in the number of homes throughout the Hills plus increased building in cities, both in the Hills and on the periphery, has meant increased pressure on the water table due to the number of wells draining from it. In wet years it is replenished but in dry years the water table is effected markedly; (2) Agricultural activities also play a significant role in the lowering of the water table. Land management for increased cultivation and grazing has involved intensive clearing of the valleys, with grubbing out and spraying of streamside vegetation being widespread. In addition, cattle grazing in seepage areas, along springs and floodplains, has a compacting effect that reduces flowage; (3) Erosion is a continuing problem, along with continual pressure for additional roads and highways. The total effect is a definite, marked decrease in the level of the water table throughout the Hills.

In some parts of the Hills pollution of streams is a major problem. Locally, mine wastes contribute silt and chemicals, in isolated instances in considerable quantities (i.e. Whitewood Creek); erosion in disturbed areas adds silt; agricultural activities and population pressure add organic pollutants. In spite of these factors, there are several major streams where the water quality remains relatively high. This is particularly true of streams at higher elevations, notably Castle Creek, Spearfish Creek and Beaver Creek.

Riparian vegetation is essential for stabilizing stream banks and maintaining cool water temperatures. Beaver activity and livestock and deer grazing have taken their toll of the vegetation to the point where increased water temperature due to lack of shade have made many streams marginal or unsuitable for trout. This has become a problem at lower elevations; whereas at higher elevations the cooler temperatures help. Trout are not native to the Hills. They were first introduced in the 1880's. With the gradual, but continuous, depletion in water quality, natural reproduction, except in isolated cases, is minimal. Therefore, in nearly all streams maintenance of fish populations is dependent upon stocking with hatchery-reared trout. In spite of this, trout fishing, particularly in high quality streams, remains generally good to excellent throughout the season.

Although no natural lakes occur in the Black Hills, there are several reservoirs resulting from dams constructed across major drainages. These artificial impoundments are divided into two categories according to size. Lakes that are over 100 surface acres are classified as large lakes; those that are less than 40 surface acres are small lakes. It is interesting to note that there are no intermediate sized lakes, between 40 and 100 surface acres, in the Hills.

There are only four large lakes, three of which are located in the central Hills; Pactola, Deerfield and Sheridan Lakes. The fourth, Stockade Lake, is located in Custer State Park. There are a number of small lakes. Notable among them are Roubaix and Iron Creek Lakes in the northern Hills; Horsethief Lake near Mt. Rushmore; the famous Sylvan Lake near Harney Peak and Legion, Center and Bismark Lakes in Custer State Park; Canyon Lake on the western edge of Rapid City; and Cold Brook Dam near Hot Springs. In addition, two major reservoirs are located outside the Hills proper: to the south, Angostura Reservoir south of Hot Springs and Belle Fourche Reservoir northeast of Belle Fourche, north of the Hills.

Sheridan Lake on Spring Creek has an area of 395 acres and is the most important lake in the Hills from the standpoint of recreation, absorbing approximately 25% of the total Black Hills recreational pressure . . . fishing, water skiing, swimming, and camping. Although no domestic water supplies are currently drawn from the lake it has potential for such usage, and a small amount of water is used for irrigation. The water is of high quality, with good trout-holding capacities, although plant development is excessive in and around the water; siltation has reduced the depth and water quality.

Deerfield Lake on upper Castle Creek, the highest large lake in the Hills at an elevation of 6,000 feet, has an area of 435 acres. The water quality is excellent. It is a very productive lake and has not been significantly altered by disturbances in its watershed. Dense algal blooms do not occur, but siltation is occurring. It serves as a major recreation area and is a domestic water source for Rapid City, as well as providing irrigation water for the lowlands. The outlet is controlled, providing a stable water flow for Castle Creek, below the dam.

Pactola Reservoir on Rapid Creek is the largest lake in the Hills proper, covering 800 acres. It is also an important source for both domestic and agricultural water. Although the productivity is lower than that of the other large lakes, fishing pressure is high. The water quality is high, but siltation and wastes from sewage and septic tanks of increasing numbers of homes in the area is becoming a problem. This is one of the most important recreational lakes, due to its size, depth and location.

Stockade Lake on French Creek, the fourth and smallest of the large lakes, covers an area of 128 surface acres. It has a low water quality rating, being polluted for both trout management and general recreation. During periods of severe drought the only water entering is effluent from the Custer City sewage treatment plant. During periods of high precipitation dilution and distribution of the effluent are improved by increased flushing of the lake. The combination of excess plant development in and around the water, siltation and wastes results in a typical dense algal bloom throughout the summer. In the spring and fall conditions are suitable for trout, but stagnation of water both in summer and winter, limiting the oxygen and confining trout to very narrow layers, has meant that the lake is marginal at best.

Among the small lakes, there are only three that are classified as having high water quality: Center Lake, Iron Creek

Lake and Cold Brook Dam. Although none of the small lakes is of great importance in itself, collectively they support a significant part of the recreational pressure in the Black Hills.

Pactola Lake. Photo courtesy Robert Evenson, 1977.

GLACIATION

It is generally assumed that there has been no glaciation in the Black Hills. There is no evidence to indicate that glaciers reached the Hills or immediately surrounding Plains. It is also most probable that plant life continued to exist in the Hills during glacial times, although undoubtedly the climatic conditions of the region were profoundly affected by the glaciers. This is particularly true for ice sheets that advanced to points relatively nearby. The western boundary of glaciation of the Wisconsin ice advances closely parallel the present course of the Missouri River in South Dakota. The edge at its closest point thus would have come to within approximately 150 miles of the Black Hills. It is generally assumed that this advance occurred during late Pleistocene, approximately 13,000 years B.P. (Cary substage of the Wisconsin, dated by carbon-14.)

33

The Continental ice sheets also covered northern North Dakota and northern Montana. There is also evidence of local glaciation in the Bighorn Mountains of Wyoming, a distance of approximately 150 miles to the west of the Black Hills. This glaciation occurred during the last glacial epoch.

Thus, with glacial activity to the east, north, and west, the ice sheets scribed a circular pattern forming an unglaciated pocket with the Black Hills in the center. Undoubtedly these conditions resulted in a more cool and moist climate in the Black Hills region, therefore presumably influencing the vegetation. There is evidence that at the time of the glaciers coniferous forests grew fairly close to the glacial boundary, and also that mountain forests descended to lower altitudes than at the present time. It is also probable that some of the coniferous species, including spruce, ponderosa, lodgepole and limber pines, may have grown more continuously in the areas surrounding the Black Hills. The assumption is that the conifers were forced back to the present restricted areas such as the Black Hills, Bear Lodge Mountains, and Slim Buttes with the glacial retreat and the resultant climatic change to more hot, dry conditions.

CLIMATE

The Black Hills area, located as it is near the center of North America, presents a combination of a near-perfect semi-arid Continental type of climate modified by a Mountain type, due to the elevation of the Hills above the surrounding plains. The result of this blend produces a climate that is highly variable, largely controlled by cyclonic and anticyclonic circulation of the air, and characterized in general by comparatively cold winters and warm summers, moderate precipitation, low relative humidity, rapid evaporation, and abundant sunshine. There are on record some notable exceptions in extremes both of temperature and precipitation (record high temperatures of 112°, and record low of —52°; 14 inches of rainfall in a four hour period, 6 inches in one hour).

34

The Black Hills exert a pronounced influence on the climate of the surrounding plains area—particularly to the east. The cover of the forests, especially, is thought to be an influence in helping to reduce the extremes of temperature, conserve precipitation, and restrict runoff.

The growing season ranges from an annual average of about 150 days near Rapid City to a very short season in the higher hills where there is the possibility of freezing temperatures every month of the year.

The winters are relatively mild, with the mean monthly temperatures for the months of December, January, and February among the warmest in South Dakota, due to the protection of the Black Hills, the frequent occurrence of Chinook winds, and the fact that the winter tracks of Arctic air masses usually pass east of Rapid City. Cold waves can be expected occasionally and one or more blizzards may occur each winter. A rather severe blizzard in which visibility is held to near zero for 24 hours or more can be expected every three or four years.

Spring is characterized by unsettled conditions. Wide variations usually occur in temperatures and snow may fall as late as May or occasionally even in June. Although the total snowfall is normally light, except at higher elevations, the heaviest snows are expected in the spring with the greatest monthly average occurring in March.

Summer days are normally warm with cool, comfortable nights. Nearly all the summer precipitation occurs as thunderstorms. Hail is often associated with the more severe thunderstorms, with the possibility of resultant damage to vegetation.

Autumn, which usually begins soon after the first of September, is characterized by mild, balmy days and cool invigorating mornings and evenings, with freezing temperatures at night. Autumn weather normally extends into November, and frequently into December. A typical autumn might offer six to eight weeks of beautiful "Indian Summer" weather.

Generally speaking, the Hills can be divided into two separate climatic zones, the "Northern Hills" and the "Southern Hills" types. Although there is no absolute distinction as to these different areas, there are sufficient differences in overall weather patterns, both winter and summer, to warrant their separation in descriptions of the climate. Moreover, residents of the area recognize these distinctions readily. The Northern type covers an area that extends from the northern limit of the Hills in the Deadwood-Lead vicinity to Spearfish and west to the Limestone plateau—south to approximately Deerfield in Castle Valley. The Southern type covers an area extending from the Deerfield region south and east through Hill City, the Harney Peak area, Custer, the State Park, Wind Cave National Park and on to the Hot Springs region and west. The two regions are divided about equally on either side of a line extending west from Rapid City. The "northern zone" is typically cooler, has heavier snowfalls, and more thunderstorms with resultant higher annual precipitation, (29 inches in the Deadwood-Lead area), more days with cloudy conditions and more gusty winds. The "southern zone," by contrast, is generally warmer, both summer and winter, has less snow and rain, total precipitation averaging lower (19.3 inches in Custer), more days of clear sunny weather and less wind. The average length of the growing season in Deadwood is 107 days while that of Hot Springs is 142. Thus there are some important gross climatic differences that influence the total balance of the Black Hills and are in turn reflected in the biological complexes of the region, including vegetation patterns.

Annual precipitation ranges from 14 to 17 inches in the adjacent Plains to 29 inches at the higher elevations in the Black Hills proper. Records of the Deadwood weather station reveal an average precipitation of 29.99 inches for the reporting period up to 1930 and for the 10 year period of 1951-1960 it averaged 28.46 inches. For all reporting stations approximately 65 to 75 percent falls from April through September. Normally, summer precipitation is in the form of sudden thundershowers. Total winter snowfall averages from 20 to 30 inches in the Plains to 100 or more inches at the higher elevations. The maximum annual snowfall for the Black Hills was 191.5 inches in 1919 recorded at Harvey's ranch in Lawrence County (elevation 6282 ft.). Although official records were not kept for many years, recent records for Deerfield in the west-central Hills indicate an average annual snowfall of 134.5 inches. Characteristically the snow melts and the ground is bare between storms so that snow depth does not tend to accumulate except on the north slopes of the higher hills, the peaks and at higher elevations on the Limestone Plateau.

Based on records from 11 stations, well distributed throughout the region, and of from 20 to 72 years duration, the mean annual temperature for the Black Hills is 45.6° F. The average absolute range in temperature for the region is 141°. The highest temperature on record was 112° at Belle Fourche in the north and at Hot Springs in the south. The lowest temperatures recorded are —52° at Custer, —42° at Belle Fourche, —41° at Hot Springs and —40° at Lead. The mean daily maximum and minimum temperatures are fairly uniform for several reporting stations: Belle Fourche max. . . . 60.3°, min. . . . 31.4; Custer max. . . . 55.8, min. . . . 26.0; Deadwood max. . . . 56.9, min. . . . 30.4; Hot Springs max. . . . 62.5, min. . . . 33.3; Rapid City max. . . . 58.6, min. . . . 35.2. Extremes of temperature are not so great in the Black Hills as on the adjacent plains although rapid changes are not infrequent. At Rapid City the greatest change in temperature for a 24 hour period is 64° F; in a two hour period the temperature dropped from 40° F to —13° F (January 12, 1911). July is usually the warmest month and January the coldest.

High winds are not infrequent in the Hills especially in the spring and early fall, although the velocities are normally less than on the plains, where the dessicating effect of the dry winds is an important factor in plant growth. Tornadoes are extremely rare in the Hills although there are records of them having occurred in at least three localities; in the vicinity of Jewell Cave, in Rapid City and near Cheyenne Crossing. On June 25, 1975, 11 tornadoes were reported as having caused some damage in separate localities in the Hills area, although none were considered as major. Hailstorms occur with some regularity during the summer months.

There are a number of extreme weather conditions that have been recorded for the Black Hills area; however, none can surpass the tragic and infamous Rapid City (Black Hills) storm and flood of the night of June 9 and early morning of June 10, 1972. "It will long be remembered not only for the tragic loss of life and property but also as a hydrologic event of such magnitude and rarity that the recurrence interval is more than ordinarily problematical."* The storm covered an area of approximately 20 by 40 miles including watersheds in the Rapid City vicinity, and parts of Pennington, Meade and Lawrence Counties, extending from Bear Butte Creek on the north to Iron Creek, a tributary of Battle Creek, on the South. A maximum intensity of nearly 6 inches of rain per hour was reached at the peak of the storm. The following summary is taken from *Storm Data and Unusual Weather Phenomena,* U.S. Department of Commerce, National Oceanic and Atmospheric Administration, Environmental Data Service, Vol. 14, No. 6, Asheville, North Carolina, June 1972.

"Heavy rains of up to 14 inches over the east slopes of the northern Black Hills causes flash flooding in the area. Much of the area from Keystone to Sturgis received 6 inches or more of rain. Most of the rain fell in a period of 4 hours or less. Most of the damage occurred in Rapid City but other areas along the creeks that drain the east slopes of the northern Black Hills also suffered flood damage. The damage was compounded by the collapse of Canyon Lake dam located just above Rapid City and caused a wall of water to rush down Rapid Creek through the city. Other creeks along which extensive damage was reported were: Bear Butte Creek which flows through Sturgis; Battle Creek, and Grizzly Creek, which flows through Keystone, Spring Creek which flows through Rockerville, Box Elder Creek which flows through Piedmont. There were 237 deaths with 5 missing and presumed dead. A total of 2,932 persons were injured with 118 hospitalized. Flood damage was over 100 million dollars. There were 750 homes destroyed with major damage to 2,261 homes and minor damage to 3,117 homes. It was

*Orr, Howard K. 1973. *The Black Hills (South Dakota) Flood of June 1972: Impacts and Implications.* U.S.D.A. For. Serv. Gen. Tech. Rep. RM-2, 12 p. Rocky Mt. For. and Range Expt. Sta., Ft. Collins, Colo.

estimated between one to two thousand cars were damaged beyond repair. A total of 6,570 families suffered losses. Damage to crops was minor compared to the property damage."

Limestone Plateau, looking north from a point near Mile High Mt., west of Custer. Photo courtesy of Robert Evenson, 1977.

Part II

HISTORICAL INFORMATION

EARLY HISTORY AND EXPLORATIONS
INDIANS, GOLD AND THE OPENING OF THE HILLS
NATIVE AMERICANS
THE DAKOTA (SIOUX) INDIANS

"In the beginning the Great Spirit gave the prairies rare gifts. The mirage, the warm rains of springtime, the grasses, the flowers, the buffalo, the village by the river and the children basking in the sun. Happy were we then, Oh my people! But from the East a white warrior came and with a mighty arrow wounded the prairie.

"And the grasses and the flowers withered, and the herds and the villages melted away.

"Melted, Oh my People! as the snow melts before the Chinook.

"In time the wound healed; but a scar was left. A long white scar across the prairie's breast."

A Sioux version of the "Western Trail" written by Robert V. Carr in his book of poems entitled *Black Hills Ballads*. 1902. The Reed Publishing Co., Denver, Colorado, p. 123; it also appears in Carr's *Cow Boy Lyrics*. 1908. W.B. Conkey Co., Chicago, Illinois.

45

EARLY HISTORY AND EXPLORATIONS

Most early literary and historical accounts of the settlement of the western part of the continent present a distorted viewpoint. The typical account begins with the Anglo-Americans crossing the Alleghenies and Appalachians in the mid 1700's, thus signalling the opening of the west. Actually, large segments of the western mountains, plains, and southwest desert area had been explored much earlier. Therefore, in order to gain a more accurate perspective of "how the west was won," one should take a broader-based "continental approach." In fact, early explorations began with the incursion of the Spanish explorers into the southwest in the early 1500's. Later the French voyageurs came from the northeast initially exploring the Great Lakes area. Their probings led them along major river drainages, including the Mississippi and St. Croix areas of present day Minnesota and Wisconsin. There is evidence that they ultimately came to the Missouri River and followed it upstream toward what was to become Dakota Territory. There seems to have been, according to several accounts, a quest for discovering a route to the mythical, but later to be verified, big water far to the west.

There are no records indicating that any white man actually saw the Black Hills until the French explorers Francois and Louis-Joseph Verendrye evidently were in the area in late 1742 and early 1743. Their route was traced, following the discovery of the Verendrye plate near Ft. Pierre, South Dakota in 1913. Apparently they reached as far west as Bear Butte near present day Sturgis, South Dakota, exploring that region in January 1743.* There is nothing to indicate that they entered the Black Hills proper, however.

The earliest documented record of the exploration of the region (Black Hills) is found in the Journals of Lewis & Clark, 1804-1806.** Near the mouth of the Cheyenne River they met the French trader Jean Valle and later, at the Knife River, Bap-

---

*Deland, Charles E. 1914. *The Verendrye Explorations and Discoveries.* South Dakota Historical Collections, Vol. VII: pp. 90-323.

**Thwaites, Reuben Gold, editor. 1904. *Original Journals of Lewis & Clark 1804-1806.* Dodd, Mead & Co., New York.

tiste LePage joined the expedition. Both Valle and LePage had been trapping in the Black Hills (the record refers to them as Black Mountains), and were able to describe the region. This is probably the first published material relating to the Black Hills.

The next record is that of the American Fur Company's expedition to the Columbia River led by Wilson P. Hunt in 1811. Hunt's expedition skirted the Hills to the north. They came within view of them, but they did not enter the Hills proper. However, Hunt's report did include a description of the Hills, as it reads, "an extensive chain, lying about a hundred

miles east of the Rocky Mountains, and stretching in a northeast direction from the south fork of the Nebraska, or Platte river, to the great north bend of the Missouri. The Sierra or ridge of the Black Hills, in fact, forms the dividing line between the waters of the Missouri and those of the Arkansas and the Mississippi, and gives rise to the Cheyenne, the Little Missouri, and several tributary streams of the Yellowstone.

"The wild recesses of these hills, like those of the Rocky Mountains are retreats and lurking places for broken and predatory tribes, and it was among them that the remnant of the Cheyenne tribe took refuge, as has been stated, from their conquering enemies, the Sioux.

"The Black Hills are chiefly composed of sandstone, and in many places are broken into savage cliffs and precipices, and present the most singular and fantastic forms; sometimes resembling towns and castellated fortresses."*

Records indicate that the first white party to actually enter the Hills was under the command of Jedediah Smith in October, 1823. This group of 12 "mountain men" crossed the Cheyenne river near the mouth of Beaver Creek, through Buffalo Gap, and continued on west through the Southern Black Hills. James Clyman, secretary of the party described the area. . . . "At

length we arrived at the foot of the black Hills which rises in very slight elevation above the common plain. . . . we

---

*Irving, Washington. 1836. *Astoria, or Anecdotes of an Enterprise Beyond the Rocky Mountains.* Vol. II, p. 91.

entered a pleasant undulating pine Region cool and re-freshing so different from the hot dusty plains we have been so long passing over and here we found hazlenuts and ripe plumbs a luxury not expected. . . ."* Truly a significant landmark in Black Hills history, this is the only account, by a participant, of the white man's first positively recorded and documented entry into the Black Hills. Clyman's record is very colorful, reporting such interesting items as a grizzly bear charging down and ripping off Jedediah Smith's ear and where Black Harris and Bill Sublette found a "putrified" forest with "putrified" trees on which "putrified" birds sang "putrified" songs.

Cleophas O'Harra in his paper on the Custer Expedition of 1874 states: "Notwithstanding this early acquaintance with the Black Hills accurate information concerning the region was for many years extremely meagre. White men occasionally hunted and trapped among the foothills and along the streams leading out therefrom and it is definitely known that there was a fur trading post near the mouth of the Belle Fourche river and another on White river near the mouth of Wounded Knee creek as early as about 1828. The American Fur Company in 1835 sent two men named Kiplin and Sabille from Ft. Laramie to Bear Butte and the northern Black Hills, to persuade the Indians living there to come out and hunt and live in their vicinity along the north fork of the Platte. They were successful and returned with more than one hundred lodges of Oglala Sioux under Chief Bull Bear."**

The next report of early explorers is that of Dr. Frederick Wislizenus. He refers to his passage through the Black Hills in 1839. However, it is doubtful that he actually was in this region. His descriptions indicate that he may have been southwest of the Hills and probably in the Laramie Mountains of Wyoming instead.

---

*Camp, C. L. (ed.). 1928. *James Clyman, American Frontiersman 1792-1881.* A. H. Clark Co., Cleveland.

** O'Harra, Cleophas C. 1929. *Custer's Black Hills Expedition of 1874.* Black Hills Engineer Vol. 17, pp. 221-286.

There followed a period of time when mountain men worked the Hills and Badlands, hunting and trapping. They occasionally would bring back fossil and mineral specimens, and descriptions of such findings began to filter back east. Occasional papers and reports of such activities appeared, including the first published map of the Badlands in 1852. The map included a very poor representation of a part of the Black Hills. Its major contribution probably was that it attracted a great deal of interest and paved the way for additional investigation of the area.

The next accounts are those of the military explorations, the first of which was the "Sioux expedition," led by General W. F. Harney in 1855, which explored the territory from Ft. Pierre to Ft. Laramie.* Lt. G. K. Warren, Dr. F. V. Hayden, Mr. J. H. Snowden and Mr. W. P. Blake helped accumulate a large amount of data on the geological and physical features of the Hills and surrounding area as well as information on routes through the region, the major rivers, weather data, and general descriptions. Lt. Warren served as the topographical engineer on this expedition, and, continuing this work in 1856-57, he explored the routes through the Black Hills and most of the major rivers in the entire region. Lt. Warren actually was in the Hills for the purpose of locating the most strategic place for a military post, in spite of the fact that Gen. Harney had concluded a treaty with the Indians in 1855 which forbade white men to travel through Indian country except along the Platte and White Rivers between Forts Pierre and Laramie. Dr. F. V. Hayden spent many months studying the geology of western South Dakota. As a matter of interest, he is reported to be the first white man to climb Bear Butte. Warren and Hayden beginning from Ft. Laramie in 1857, conducted a rapid reconnaissance of the Black Hills, encountering strenuous opposition but no actual fighting from Indians as they entered the Southern Hills. However, the encounter forced the party to follow alternate routes from those originally planned. In spite of the Indian problem and the circuitous route they were forced to take, "this

*Warren, Lt. G. K. 1875. *Preliminary Report of Explorations in Nebraska and Dakota in the years 1855-56-57,* p. 19. (Gov. Print. Off., Washington).

expedition yielded our first real knowledge of the topography and drainage of the region and it outlined in a fairly good way the varied nature of the sedimentary rocks flanking the main uplift. The investigations, followed by important publications accompanied by geographical and geological maps, proved to be unusually accurate, considering the hurried manner in which they had to be carried on, and, until after the coming of Custer, all subsequent maps of the region were based on this work."*

In 1859, Captain W. F. Raynolds and Dr. Hayden led an expedition to the Black Hills. Based on information gathered on this expedition and on additional studies he carried out intermittently until 1866, Dr. Hayden released his geological report of the Black Hills in 1869.** This work included valuable data in regard to the geology and paleontology of the region and provided considerable information about the Black Hills. Concerning the importance of the Black Hills region as a field for geological study Dr. Hayden says: "The Black Hills of Dakota

will form one of the most interesting studies on this continent. There is so much regularity in the upheaval that all obscurity is removed and all the formations known in the west are revealed in zones or belts around the granitic nucleus in their fullest development. A careful detailed topographical and geological survey of this range would be

a most valuable contribution to science." Thus, although military expeditions had a specific purpose, a great deal of scientific information was secured because someone, fortunately, had the foresight to assign scientists and naturalists to accompany the expeditions.

INDIANS, GOLD AND THE OPENING OF THE HILLS

During the 1860's and early 1870's a number of factors led to the rapid opening of the Black Hills. Probably the most signifi-

---

*O'Harra, Cleophas C. 1929. *Custer's Black Hills Expedition of 1824.* Black Hills Engineer Vol. XVII. pp. 221-286.

**Hayden, F. V. 1869. *Geological Report of the Explorations of the Yellowstone and Missouri Rivers under the direction of Capt. W. F. Raynolds in 1859-60.* Gov. Print. Off., Washington.

cant development was the report from many sources that there was gold in the Hills. Rumors of gold began to filter through to the east as early as the dates when the first white men came into the area. More pressure from white prospectors and increasing encounters with the Indians led to the Powder River expedition of 1865, a military force of three divisions, led by Brigadier General Connor (Ft. Laramie), James Sawyers, Colonel Nelson Cole (Omaha), and Lt. Col. Samuel Walker (Ft. Kearney), which passed northward around the Black Hills to pacify and "impress" the Indians. Very little was reported from this expedition, probably because of the Civil War problem.

The rumors of gold began to intensify, and the prospector's desire to actively invade the Hills became overwhelming. The obstacle of the Indians' ownership of the area stood in the way. Obviously, the Indians were very much aware of the difficulties likely to ensue if the white man came into their country. They were particularly protective of their most favored sacred ground, the Paha Sapa. Thus the stage was set for General George A. Custer's expedition from Ft. Abraham Lincoln in July and August, 1874. His orders were to organize an expedition for "the purpose of reconnoitering a route to the Black Hills and of exploring their hither unattained mountainous interior."

The expedition was highly publicized and described as successful and it immediately proved an outstanding event in the development of the Black Hills. Many accounts were published in the popular press. From that point on, the Custer expedition, and events leading up to the famous, or infamous, Battle of the Little Big Horn, have probably been given more publicity and notoriety than any other single event in American history.

Captain William Ludlow accompanied the expedition as chief engineer, Professor N. H. Winchell as geologist, Professor A. B. Donaldson, assistant, Mr. George Bird Grinnell as naturalist (zoology and paleontology), Mr. L. H. North, assistant, Dr. J. W. Williams, chief medical officer and botanist, Mr. W. H. Illingworth as photographer and William Ellery Curtis and others as newspaper correspondents. Charles Reynolds, the well-known guide was with the expedition, as were also two miners, Horatio Nelson Ross and William T. McKay. General George

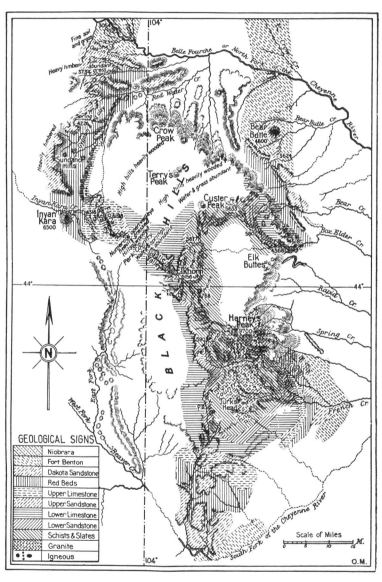

Winchell's Geological Map of the Black Hills, prepared during the Custer Expedition of 1874, reproduced in several Black Hills publications.

A. Forsyth and Col. Fred Grant (son of President U. S. Grant) were officers with the military forces. A military band, something new in western plains travel, was also a part of the organization (this fact of itself has led to a great deal of speculation and comment). The leader of the Indian Scouts was Bloody Knife.

The expedition traveled approximately 600 miles in 60 days. They returned with many photographs and recorded observations on the natural history of the area . . . also with proof of the presence of gold (see note below).

In the recorded accounts by various members of the expedition frequent reference is made to the luxuriance of the vegetation growing in the Black Hills. The official description (Custer) of one valley in the Limestone area reads as follows: "Every step of our march that day was amid flowers of the most exquisite colors and perfume. So luxuriant in growth were they that men plucked them without dismounting from the saddle. . . . It was a strange sight to glance back at the advancing columns of cavalry and behold the men with beautiful bouquets in their hands, while the headgear of the horses was decorated with wreaths of flowers fit to crown a queen of May. Deeming it a most fitting appellation, I named this Floral Valley. General Forsyth, at one of our halting places, plucked 17 beautiful flowers, belonging to different varieties, and within a space of 20 feet square. The same evening, while seated at the mess table, one of the officers called attention to the carpet of flowers strewn under our feet, and it was suggested that it be determined how many different flowers could be plucked without leaving our seat at dinner table. Seven beautiful varieties were thus gathered. Professor Donaldson, the botanist of the ex-

Note:
The Illingworth photographs and their modern counterparts have recently been published (1974) in two books that are of particular interest to anyone desiring information on the Black Hills and the Custer episode: Donald Progulske's *"Yellow Ore, Yellow Hair and Yellow Pine"*, (1974, published by SDSU Agricultural Extension Service, Brookings, South Dakota), and Herbert Krause and Gary Olson's *"Prelude to Glory"*, (1974, Brevet Press, Sioux Falls, South Dakota). The complete history of gold in the Black Hills is exceptionally well-presented by Watson Parker in his book *"Gold in the Black Hills"*, (1966 Univ. Oklahoma Press).

pedition, estimated the number of flowers in bloom in Floral Valley at 50, while an equal number of varieties had bloomed, or were yet to bloom. The number of trees, shrubs, and grasses was estimated at 25, making the total flora of the valley embrace 125 species."*

As a direct result of the authentication of gold in the Hills, authorities with the Bureau of Indian Affairs decided that it was necessary to determine more accurately how much gold there was. Subsequently, acting under the direct authority of the Secretary of War, the Bureau ordered the Newton-Jenney geological survey party to the Hills in 1875. Walter P. Jenney & Henry Newton, with fifteen assistants, escorted by four hundred soldiers under the command of Lt. Colonel Richard I. Dodge, spent approximately five months in the Hills. For various reasons the party did not find much gold, and Jenney sent frequent letters and reports describing his rather meager findings. The final report of the expedition was published in 1880. Meanwhile, however, neither the miners nor the settlers of the frontier towns were discouraged . . . newspapers encouraged prospectors to seek gold in the Hills. The Federal government, as a result, experienced great difficulty in keeping prospectors out of the area—which was Sioux reservation land. The end result was the "opening" of the Black Hills.

There are a number of early explorations and expeditions that were either primarily or secondarily for the purpose of collecting biological information, the majority of which were historical in nature. A listing and summary of these is included in part III, Biological Information, for those persons desiring this information (see pages 79-80).

"NATIVE AMERICANS"

The natural history of any area would be incomplete without an account of the native peoples who have inhabited it. Al-

---

This reference can be found in many publications, including:
*Custer, G. A. *Opening the Black Hills, Custer's Report.* South Dakota Historical Collections 7 (1914):583-591. Kingsbury, *History of Dakota Territory,* 1:885-888. McFarling, *Exploring the Northern Plains,* pp. 317-325. O'Harra, *Custer's Expedition of 1874,* pp. 268-281, and others.

though many cultures have played roles in the shaping of early South Dakota history, the most colorful and perhaps the most significant from the historical viewpoint is that of the Dakota (Sioux) Indians for which the original territory, and finally two states, were named. Moreover, the Teton (Lakota) Sioux (western South Dakota division) were the group that were the dominant force in shaping the history of the Black Hills area, at least since approximately 1800. Thus, the major portion of this account will deal with the Tetons. However, a summary of the Indian history of the state is included by way of introduction to place the entire historical development of the area in its proper perspective.

The term *native Americans* may be a misnomer since early man apparently migrated to the new world from Asia; however, the term is used in a generic sense to identify American Indians. There are many theories as to the routes taken in migration as early man came to North America. Perhaps the most widely accepted among anthropologists is that man came across a Bering Straits land bridge from Siberia. The evidence reveals that one of the migration routes came through Alaska, Canada, and into the United States east of the Rockies to Montana and Wyoming and Colorado. This would place early man in the Black Hills area.

There are many confusing factors involved in attempting to establish actual dates for the earliest cultures on the continent. There are archeological records (skeletons, scrapers, choppers, etc.) from many different localities that have been dated, but generally the evidence is incomplete or inconclusive. Included in this group are sites whose dates range from approximately 17,000 to over 40,000 years B.P. The 40,000 plus figures are based on two documented records: (1) a child's skeleton recorded from the vicinity of Taber, Alberta, Canada,* and (2) a skull identified as Del Mar man originally found near La Jolla, California, dated 48,000 years old - - - reported in *Science* in

---

*Stalker, M. A. 1969. *Geology and Age of Early Man Site at Taber, Alberta.* American Antiquity. Vol. 34, No. 4, p. 428.

1974.* One time estimate, not well-documented, suggests that man may date as far back as 60,000 years in America. However, this has been seriously questioned by most authorities. One of the difficulties is to correlate these date records with the glaciers, and the dates that corridors would have been open between ice sheets to allow migration through them.

However, there is general agreement among authorities that man was definitely established on the continent by at least 15,000 years ago. Certainly by 10,000 B.C. (12,000 B.P.) a culture had developed with no counterpart in the old world and had spread throughout the new world, both north and south. The people of this time period and up to approximately 4,500 years B.P. are generally referred to as the Paleo-Indians, or the Big-game Hunters. Traditionally, the culture was viable for about 5,000 years. These people were classified as hunters-gatherers with primarily a big-game hunting tradition. There is no evidence that they owned domestic dogs or horses. With the extinction of most of their big game animals—their subsistence base eliminated—the culture apparently migrated from this region.

Following the Paleo-Indian cultures which inhabited all the Plains States, archeological evidence indicates that a more advanced culture emerged—the Plains archaic culture (Fig. 4). These people engaged in a generalized foraging subsistence, hunting but also utilizing plants, as evidenced by grinding stones that have been found with their "remains."

At about the time of Christ, a major change apparently occurred in the cultural pattern of the people of this region, the introduction of agriculture—actually garden farming, including the raising of corn, beans and squash. This indicates that they probably had some previous contact with the Indians of the southwest. This culture was of the Plains-Woodlands tradition. There are many prominent burial mounds of this culture remaining in Eastern South Dakota.

Between 800-1000 A.D. the initial Middle Missouri tradition emerged. These were the first village-farming cultures. Their

---

*Bada, Jeffrey L., Roy A. Schroeder and George F. Carter, 1974. *New Evidence for The Antiquity of Man in North America Deduced from Aspartic Acid Racemization.* Science Vol. 184, No. 4138, pp. 791-793.

56

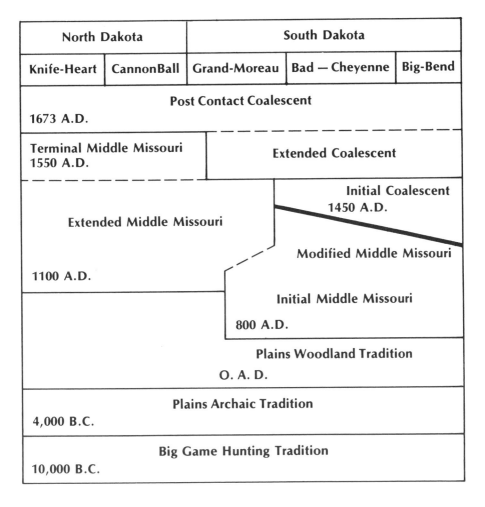

North Dakota		South Dakota		
Knife-Heart	CannonBall	Grand-Moreau	Bad — Cheyenne	Big-Bend

Post Contact Coalescent
1673 A.D.

Terminal Middle Missouri
1550 A.D.

Extended Coalescent

Extended Middle Missouri

Initial Coalescent
1450 A.D.

Modified Middle Missouri

1100 A.D.

Initial Middle Missouri

800 A.D.

Plains Woodland Tradition
O. A. D.

Plains Archaic Tradition
4,000 B.C.

Big Game Hunting Tradition
10,000 B.C.

PREHISTORIC CULTURES OF THE DAKOTAS
(Prepared by the W. H. Over Dakota Museum,
The University of South Dakota, Vermillion)

Figure 4. A summary of the cultures that have inhabited the Dakotas, indicating the river drainage system along which they lived.

57

antecedents initially came from the east, migrating along river routes. As they reached the region that included Dakota Territory they followed the Missouri from south to north. These people were probably the ancestors of the Mandan (Archaic Mandan).

Approximately 1500 A.D. additional cultural advancements occurred among the people living in the Dakotas. They were to be identified as the Initial Coalescent and Extended Coalescent traditions. These traditions included the Mandan, Hidatsa (Gros Ventres) and Arikara (Ree). These people built circular earth houses and are believed to be the major mound builders in the Dakotas. They are well known because of the large number of archaeological excavations that have been completed along the Missouri River.

At the height of the Extended Coalescent tradition well over 100 sites were occupied on both sides of the Missouri between the present North Dakota-South Dakota border and the mouth of the White River, with additional sites occupied as far south as the Nebraska line. Generally, the Arikara occupied the lower portion of the river, below the Big Bend of the Missouri and the Mandan were further north. In 1775 Truteau* reported that the Arikara told him that in about 1760 they numbered 20,000 people.

Apparently smallpox epidemics took their toll of these people. These epidemics reportedly occurred between 1772 and 1780, destroying 4/5 of the total population. Added to this type of catastrophe, the Sioux, as they gained in strength and numbers, exerted increased pressure on them and forced them continually north. By the time Lewis and Clark came to this portion of the Missouri in 1804, there were only 8 occupied villages in the entire Middle Missouri Valley (North and South Dakota). These included three Arikara towns a short distance above the Grand River in South Dakota, two Mandan and three Hidatsa settlements in the vicinity of the Knife river in North Dakota. The Arikara abandoned the last of their villages in 1832 and settled in a deserted Mandan village near Ft. Clark. In 1837 a major

---

*Truteau, J. B. "Journals". First part in *American Historical Review,* 1914; Vol. 19, No. 2, Second part in *Missouri Historical Society Collection,* Vol. 4 (St. Louis, 1913).

smallpox epidemic swept up the Missouri and over the Plains killing thousands of Indians. All three groups of the circular house builders were nearly exterminated. By 1862 only one community remained of the Missouri river villages (Garrison dam area). All downstream villages were abandoned permanently.

There were other groups of Indians, at varying intervals, that drifted west across the Dakotas. Among them, probably the most colorful were the Cheyenne. Originally an agricultural tribe, they adopted a horse and buffalo-based culture and developed into one of the most powerful Northern Great Plains tribes. They were forced west by the Chippewa and Sioux, ultimately settling in the Black Hills area, and on the Great Plains of Wyoming and Montana. They controlled the area to the north and west of the Black Hills.

There are many traditions and legends that associate the Cheyenne with Bear Butte, near Sturgis, South Dakota, to the northeast of the Black Hills proper. Bear Butte was, and is, the Cheyenne's Sacred Mountain, Noah'wus, for it was here that their supreme deity, Maheo (Maiyu), gave the four Sacred Arrows to their cultural hero, Sweet Medicine. One legend recalls the story of how the Cheyenne acquired the arrows:

"Somewhere in the Black Hills is a very high butte, and on the side of that butte is a big, flat, thick rock. Sweet Medicine and his wife went toward that rock; and when they were close to it, the rock moved to one side, and beyond it they saw an opening and a room. They went in. The first thing his wife saw after they had gone into the room was a coyote skin, beyond it they saw four arrows lying side by side, feathered with large hawk feathers and the arrows all pointing the same way. A little beyond these were four more arrows, lying with the heads all pointing the same way; these were feathered with eagle feathers. A mysterious man (maiyu) was there, who said to Sweet Medicine, 'Which arrows do you like, the arrows with the gray hawk feathers, or those with eagle feathers?' Sweet Medicine answered,

59

'I like better those with eagle feathers.' "* The sacred arrows are symbolic of the gift given by the creator whereby he shares his power with his people. They are the channel through which Maheo's supernatural life flows into Cheyenne lives. The arrows are the continuing means by which the people are united with the creator. The arrows, on Cheyenne testimony, still exist, carefully protected by the Southern Cheyenne in Oklahoma. Thus it is that, periodically, the Cheyenne return to Bear Butte to renew themselves through the Ceremony of the Four Arrows. In recent years the ceremonies have occurred in midsummer and are accompanied by several days of fasting and rituals. (For further details see Powell** or Sandoz***).

Prior to the Cheyenne, other Indians tribes lived in the Black Hills area. The Kiowa lived there for some time before being succeeded by the Sutaio and Cheyenne. The Sutaio may have been the "Chousa" band of Cheyenne of whom Perrin du Lac (1805) heard. They were probably close to the Cheyenne in their migrations from Minnesota to the Missouri River and beyond. At any rate they lived side by side in the region eastward of the Black Hills for some time and they finally united there into one body, the Sutaio taking their place as one band in the Cheyenne tribal camping circle.****

The Arapaho Indians, according to tradition, also lived for a long time in the neighborhood of the Black Hills, but after they crossed the Missouri they were most closely identified with northeastern Wyoming. In addition, the Ponca and Omaha Tribes also lived briefly in the Dakotas prior to the Sioux dominance, finally settling in northeastern Nebraska. Later, following the establishment of the reservations, the Winnebago, after

---

*Case, Leland, in chapter II of Roderick Peattie's *The Black Hills.* Vanguard Press, Inc., New York, p. 444.

**Powell, Peter J. 1969. *Sweet Medicine: The Continuing Role of The Sacred Arrows, The Sun Dance, and The Sacred Buffalo Hat in Northern Cheyenne History.* University of Oklahoma Press, 2 Vols. 935 pages.

***Sandoz, Mari. 1969. *Cheyenne Autumn.* Avon Books, New York. 336 pages.

****Swanton, John R. 1953. *The Indians Tribes of North America.* Bureau of American Ethnology. Bull. 145. U.S. Government Printing Office.

leaving Minnesota in 1862, lived for a time on the Crow Creek Reservation.

THE DAKOTA (SIOUX) INDIANS

Probably because they exerted the greatest influence of all Indian groups on the historical development of the Plains, the Sioux have been identified with Indian life in the Dakotas throughout the recorded history of the area, certainly since approximately 1700. As Royal Hassrick writes, "For many people the Sioux, as warriors and as buffalo hunters, have become the symbol of all that is Indian—colorful figures endowed with great fortitude and powerful vision. They were the heroes of the Great Plains in the days of heroes and they were the villains, too. Properly they have been the subject of much writing."* - - - Actually they were relatively late in settling in this area, following the earlier migration of the Mandan, Arikara and Hidatsa. The early record of the Sioux is obscure, but they undoubtedly had a southeastern origin (North Carolina and other states). They most likely were an agricultural type initially, and were continually pushed westward by increased settlement in the east. There is definite evidence that they resided in the region of the western Great Lakes in the 1600's. From this point in time the record is more definite, although it is impossible to trace the precise migration routes followed by the Sioux as they moved from the Great Lakes area, through Minnesota and ultimately into Dakota Territory. There are many reasons for this: (1) the different tribes and bands did not follow the same routes, (2) they migrated at different times, (3) by the time they were permanently settled in Dakota, approximately two centuries had passed, (4) no written historical records were ever maintained by them, (5) they gradually lost most of the memories of their old homelands which is not unusual in an oral tradition, (6) there are many interpretations of their history and this has confused the issue. Thus information is sketchy at best. The evidence that

---

*Hassrick, Royal B. 1964. *The Sioux, Life and Customs of a Warrior Society.* University of Oklahoma Press, Norman, Oklahoma. 337 pp.

is available is circumstantial and is based on reports, records and maps of the early explorers and fur traders that came into contact with them. One important type of evidence is the location points, indicated in early French journals and maps, of the Trading Fairs or "Rendezvous" where the Indians came to trade furs for eastern goods and guns. The "Rendezvous" locations can be used to trace the movements of the Sioux, at least indirectly. In addition, picture records were kept, called winter counts, that also provide some aid in tracing history and migrations. The winter count was usually a colored pictograph painted on a buffalo robe or tanned deer hide, each picture representing the event by which that particular year, or winter, as the Sioux called it, was to be remembered.

In order to understand and properly interpret the history of the Sioux it is necessary to distinguish the three major Divisions (tribes) that comprised the Dakota Nation, although they all belonged to one linguistic group, together with several other tribes. There were significant dialectic, cultural, geographic and historical distinctions that separated the three tribes: (1) the Santee Sioux, the Eastern Division, speaking the Dakota dialect (2) the Yankton (Wiciyela) Sioux, the Middle Division, speaking the Nakota dialect and (3) the Teton Sioux (Titonwan . . . Plains dwellers), the Western Division, speaking the Lakota dialect. Within each of the three tribes were a number of subgroups called bands or clans. There were four such subgroups in the Santee tribe: Mdewakontonwan, Wahpekute, Sisseton and Wahpeton. The Yankton tribe included two subgroups, the Yankton and Yanktonai. The Teton Sioux tribe was the largest, consisting of seven subgroups: the Oglala, Brule (Sichangus or "burnt thighs"), Sans Arc (Itazipches or without bows"), Sihasapa (Blackfeet), Minnekonju (Miniconjous), Two Kettle (Oohenonpas) and Hunkpapa. The Oglala were the largest with the Brule next important in terms of size. Apparently at one time there occurred a separation of five of the Teton subgroups, identified collectively as the Saone, (Two Kettle, Sans Arc, Blackfeet, Miniconjous, and Hunkpapa) from the remaining two, who retained the name Tetons (Oglala and Brule). However, all seven were regrouped later when it became convenient for particular purposes. Each band (subgroup) was further sub-divided into a number of extended family hunting groups called Tiyospayes (Tiyospe). Each Tiyospaye was a completely independent unit, serving allegiance to, but not governed by, the band and tribe. The Sioux's rather fluid governmental structure and organization was based on the Tiyospaye, making the nation both flexible and cohesive. Sometimes alliances were formed among the bands for hunting purposes or other cultural activities. The chiefs were always selected within the Tiyospaye and not the band or tribe. Existence for the Sioux people was the challenging combination of individual endeavor and group enterprise. It was harassed by trial and error, frustrated by conservatism and tortured by change. The question may persist in the minds of some as to the degree to which their environment determined their adjustment and destiny; but it was undoubtedly pertinent to the Sioux nations' vigorous and rapid development on the Plains, their sheer dominance and tragic decline, all in a relatively short period of time.

All three Divisions were forced farther west . . . by pressures from continued western expansion and settlement by white man, but perhaps more particularly by the Chippewa . . . out of the western Great Lakes area and into present day Minnesota and Eastern Dakota sometime after 1600 (Fig. 5). They settled for a time near the headwaters of the Mississippi river, but were forced south in two distinct waves. The Yanktonais (including the Yanktons at this time) and Tetons (entire tribe) began their migration to south central Minnesota about 1670. These groups became identified together as the "Sioux of the West." They were so designated on the maps of French voyageurs. Sometime after 1735 the other group, the Santee, later known as the "Sioux of the East", migrated to south central Minnesota. They finally settled permanently in the general area that extends from the current locations of Blue Earth and Mankato, Minnesota, upstream along the Minnesota River as far as Lake Traverse (on the border of present day northeast South Dakota and Minnesota). The Santee remained an agricultural-hunter-gatherer culture, retaining their basic woodlands tradition.

63

SIOUX NATION: ORIGINAL SEVEN COUNCIL FIRES

"SIOUX OF THE EAST"

WAHPETON   MDEWAKANTONWAN
SISSETON   WAHPEKUTE

"SIOUX OF THE WEST"

YANKTONAI   YANKTON   TETON

Seven Subtribes of Tetons

Oglala   Blackfeet
Brule   Two Kettle
Hunkpapa   Miniconjous
Sans Arc

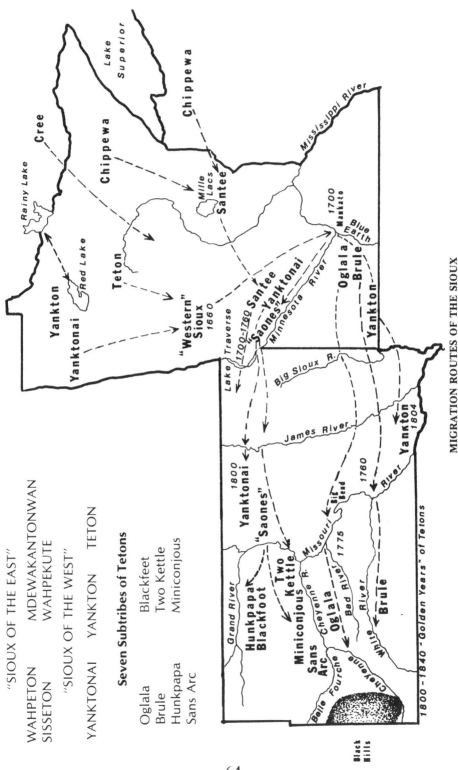

MIGRATION ROUTES OF THE SIOUX

Figure 5. A generalized map indicating the probable routes followed as the Sioux migrated from the Great Lakes area, ultimately settling in Dakota Territory.

64

The Tetons temporarily settled near what is now Sauk Rapids, Minnesota, west of the Mississippi river. This was south of the location occupied at this time by the Yanktonais. About 1770 the entire western Sioux group again moved south to the point known as the elbow bend of the Minnesota river, near Mankato. This river elbow seems to have been a "trap" . . . dividing one tribe or band after another . . . since it was here that they were forced to make a decision as to whether they should cross the river and proceed south and west, thus occupying open prairie country, or to remain on the north side of the river, follow it upstream and thus stay in the wooded country. The Dakota name for the crossing place was Oiyuwega which the first French occupants translated as the *Traverse des Sioux.* The country, included in the loop formed by the great bend of the Minnesota River at the mouth of the Blue Earth, was known to the Dakota as "Kamin" (The Bend). The first white man to see the place was Pierre Charles Le Sueur, who in September 1700, with a party of miners and soldiers, explored the Mississippi, Minnesota and Blue Earth Rivers.* The decision on crossing was critical, for it meant that it became the ultimate choice that forced a drastic change in cultural patterns or allowed them to remain as they were. For those that made the crossing it meant essentially a new way of life, changing from a woodlands tradition to a nomadic prairie-plains culture.

The Yankton separated, crossed the river and occupied the area from the Blue Earth River to the Pipestone Quarry in western Minnesota. Later, the Yankton crossed into Dakota settling in the James River basin and along the southern border of the state as far west as the Missouri River. The Yanktonais chose to follow the Minnesota River upstream, settling finally in northeastern South Dakota. The Tetons also split into two groups when they reached the river elbow area. The Brule and Oglala crossed the river and started a slow but continuous migration westward. In the early 1700's they were hunting in the prairie country west of Blue Earth as far as the valley of the James River

*Hughes, Thomas. 1929. *Old Traverse des Sioux.* Chapter II, Early History of the Crossing. Herald Publ. Co., St. Peter, Minn.

65

in Dakota. These were usually forays in small groups that drifted here and there, and they did not settle down. In the spring they took their furs to the Rendezvous or Trading Fair at the headwaters of the Minnesota River, near Big Stone Lake. The remaining five Teton bands, identified collectively as the "Saones," or Teton-Saones, did not cross the river, but migrated upstream to Lake Traverse. They remained in this area for a time (until approximately 1720), but later migrated further west to the Missouri River and north central South Dakota, thus finally forcing the Mandan and Arikara northward into North Dakota.

During the period from approximately 1700-1750 the Oglala and Brule were slowly drifting westward, changing their cultural patterns from a woodlands type of existence and becoming truly Plains Indian types. They rather rapidly changed to a basic buffalo economy. Early French chronicles, relating the first contacts with the Sioux on the Great Plains definitely associated them with the buffalo. The buffalo became more than a means of subsistence - - - providing food, clothing, shelter, and an amazing variety of tools and ceremonial objects - - - they truly were the center of their culture and way of life. The Tetons in a relatively short time commanded vast areas of the Plains wilderness; they quickly adapted hunting patterns similar to those of other Plains tribes. It was at this time that they first came into contact with the Arikara. This initial contact was not as a complete tribe, and not in any sense an invasion or war. They came in small bands, poor people, not as conquerors, but more as beggars. Gradually they gained strength as they rapidly adapted to the new way of life. It was during this general time period that the Arikara began to weaken. In the late 1700's the smallpox epidemic struck, destroying their power, and they became vulnerable to the Sioux. The Arikara were forced north to the Cheyenne River area.

It is generally accepted that the Oglala and Brule moved across the Missouri River below the Great Bend in 1775. The Oglalas soon occupied the area between the Bad and Cheyenne Rivers. The Brule settled along the White River. Subsequent to crossing the Missouri the old Teton tribe ultimately separated into the seven subgroups, the Oglala and Brule toward the South, and the Saone (the nations to the north) who now split into the five groups: Hunkpapa, Sans Arc, Miniconju, Blackfeet, and Two Kettle.

In approximately 1776 an Oglala war party led by Standing Bull roved far enough west to discover the Black Hills. During this time period, the Cheyenne Indians reported their first contact with the Sioux as being small hunting parties traveling on foot. By 1800 the Oglalas travelled regularly from the Black Hills area to the mouth of the Bad River near Ft. Pierre, trading with the French and later, the American Fur Company.

George E. Hyde, in *Red Cloud's Folk*, states: "During these years (approximately 1805-1835) the Oglala camps were almost always within sight of the Black Hills, which from a distance in the plains appeared as a faint blue shape on the horizon, but seen more at hand rose grim and black against the sky. In winter the camps were located in sheltered stream valleys close to the eastern edge of the hills, and sometimes the people went into the mountain valleys to hunt deer and elk or to cut lodge-poles; but Paha Sapa, the Black Hills, was sacred ground, the heart of Teton land, where people did not venture to camp. A whole epoch in the life of the Tetons has been lost through the failure to record in writing at an earlier date the tale of the Sioux migration to the Black Hills and their early life in that region. Here and there we catch a glimpse of the rich materials we have lost, as in the mention of the Race Track . . . (Darton's Red Valley). . . . This was a lodge trail that ran completely around the base of the Black Hills. When the Indians surrendered the Hills in 1876, they said . . . 'We give the lands as far as the Race Track' . . . The Bears Lodge Medicine Pipe Mountain, the Old Woman's Hill, the Dancer's Hill, and the Buffalo Gate . . . (Buffalo Gap) . . . behind each of these names lies a story of those early times, but most of the stories have been lost."*

Another major development, during this period of time, was the introduction of the horse to the Sioux. It is common knowl-

*Hyde, George E. 1937. *Red Cloud's Folk: A History of the Oglala Sioux*. Univ. Oklahoma Press, Norman, Okla.

edge that horses were introduced to the New World initially by the Spaniards, brought north from Mexico, then through trading, stealing and escapes the Apache, Comanche, and other Indians acquired them. Ultimately they came to the Cheyenne, who in turn traded them to the Sioux. The Arikara also possessed some horses and probably were the first to introduce them to the Sioux, but it is generally thought that the Cheyenne were their source in any quantity. The combination of the buffalo economy, the vast hunting ground available in the Plains area, and finally the horse as a rapid means of transportation, gave the Sioux the potential of developing a new and different way of life, a nomadic existence. The tipis (conical tents of animal hides stretched over wooden poles) as a movable type of housing, the travois (load-bearing platform consisting of two poles with a hide stretched between them, pulled by a horse) for transport of possessions easily and relatively quickly, and the change from a sedentary agricultural subsistence to the buffalo economy all led to a highly mobile, functional life style. Rapidly spreading to the west the Tetons soon controlled the region as far as the Black Hills and eastern Wyoming. They were destined to become the colorful prototype of the American Indian. It was small wonder that, because of the confrontations between White and Indian in this part of the country due to western expansion, the Tetons in particular became known as the notorious "light cavalry" warrior society. Because a great deal of highly publicized literature relating to the Sioux focuses particularly on the Tetons, this is the group that became widely known as "The" Sioux.

The rapid rise to power and control of such a large area in such a relatively short time (approximately 50 years) is one of the most amazing illustrations of adaptation in the history of man. In a few short years the Tetons rose from a small group of poor isolated bands to the most powerful Indian tribe on the continent. They reached their peak of cultural development during the period from approximately 1800 to 1840-50, the so-called "golden years" of the Tetons.

Being the most numerous, of the Sioux, the Tetons were also the most powerful and resistant to white invasion, producing such outstanding chiefs as Crazy Horse (Oglala), Red Cloud (Oglala . . . Although Hyde in *Red Cloud's Folk* states that his father was Lone Man, a Brule chief, he is generally regarded to have been an Oglala), Sitting Bull (Hunkpapa), Gall (Hunkpapa) and Spotted Tail (Oglala). Together with the Oglala, the Brule and Hunkpapa were the bands that caused most of the trouble for the emigrants on all the various lines of travel across the northern Plains between the Missouri and the Rocky Mountains.

Following the golden days for the Sioux came a long period of frustration, defeat and the ultimate near-collapse of a once-proud culture. The steady overwhelming incursion of the white man, disease, the near extinction of the buffalo, numerous engagements and defeats at the hands of the military, and ultimate confinement on the reservations all took their toll.

Resistance to the white man probably would have developed earlier than it did if the Sioux had possessed a different, stronger cultural organization. They persisted in following their traditional (individual band) way of life with no group organization that could cope with new problems. They were relatively patient and "were content to stand by the trails" year after year and watch the wagons roll, probably thinking that sooner or later the white man's country would be drained of its people and they would all be gone from their land . . . but the whites still came, spreading disease (smallpox, cholera, the fever), and destroying the wild game. Resentment grew for these strange unfriendly men who "didn't even bring trade goods with them," who filled the trail with their cattle, their women and children and who began seriously to threaten the Indian's way of life. The gold discovery in California brought waves of prospectors over the Plains enroute west. The problem intensified as Indians began more actively to resist. Soon they were ready to take to the warpath. (For a detailed account see James C. Olson, *Red Cloud and the Sioux Problem.*)* In 1851 a great peace council was called near what is now Laramie, Wyoming, with some

---

*Olson, James C. 1965. *Red Cloud and the Sioux Problem.* Univ. Nebraska Press, Lincoln, Nebraska. 375 pp.

10,000 northern Plains Indians, predominantly Sioux, attending. The tribes pledged peace among themselves and with the United States, and moreover, promised safe passage for whites across Indian lands. Neither side lived up to the terms of the council. Continued Indian attacks on wagon trains and settlements resulted in a military campaign against the Sioux (Brule) in 1855. This show of force so impressed the Tetons that a few years of relative peace followed. However, serious breaches of the Council agreement persisted and finally the Minnesota uprising in 1862 so alarmed the entire Sioux Nation that renewed attacks began all along the frontier trails. Then, in 1865 the Indians were further inflamed with the passage by Congress of a bill authorizing new routes to the west, passing directly through the Teton's buffalo range. Chief Red Cloud led his people in armed protest . . . for a period of time the area became practically impassable to whites. Thus, serious attempts at peace were begun and ultimately the famous Fort Laramie treaty of 1868 was negotiated. The United States government agreed to keep whites from hunting or settling on Indian territory and established a Great Sioux Reservation which included all of present day South Dakota west of the Missouri "for the absolute and undisturbed use and occupation of the Indians named herein." The government also agreed to abandon proposed trails west and to pay annuities for appropriated Indian lands. The Indians agreed to release all east river lands except for the Crow Creek, Yankton, and Sisseton Reservations previously established. By the end of the year nearly half of the Sioux were on reservations. Things remained relatively quiet for a few years. Then a series of events occurred which spelled more trouble; in 1874, gold seekers began to rush to the Black Hills area. A number of Sioux bands were allowed off reservation land to hunt buffalo in the fall of 1875. Later, they were ordered to return to the reservation, but could not travel because of the severe cold and lack of food. General George C. Crook was ordered to drive the Indians back to the reservation; subsequently he attacked the camp of Crazy Horse. The Indians escaped, but returned the following spring and scored a decisive victory over General Crook in the 1876 Battle of the Rosebud.

This defeat resulted in the Army ordering General George C. Custer and his 7th Cavalry to the area to suppress the Indians "once and for all." The famous Battle of the Little Big Horn occurred June 25, 1876. Custer's last stand was the last great Sioux victory over the Army. Following this battle, the Indians scattered and were ultimately defeated by the Army, band by band . . . finally they had no choice but to surrender and accept the terms of an 1876 agreement (it is noteworthy that this was not a treaty, as were all former settlements; the term *agreement* was specifically used) by which they relinquished not only their sacred Black Hills, but the surrounding area as well. The Indians were forced back to the reservations, largely because the massive buffalo herds were being systematically destroyed by white hunters. Without food, and under continued pressure by the Army, the chiefs surrendered one by one. Crazy Horse surrendered in 1877 and the Oglalas settled at Pine Ridge. By 1881 Sitting Bull and Gall surrendered, returning to the Standing Rock reservation.

Several years of unrest followed, probably due to the development on the reservation of the Ghost Dance religion. This religious cult began to attract public attention in 1890. The success of the movement is generally attributed to the mood of the Indians, one of utter despair. The religion and accompanying ceremonial dances were based on the revelations attributed to the prophet Wovoka (a Paiute Indian). The promise of the religion was that the Great Spirit was to return the fallen warriors, and at the same time the white people and their culture were to be destroyed by a natural cataclysm. In addition there was the promise of the replenishment of the buffalo, antelope and other game.

The Ghost Dance itself consisted of continuous ceremonial dancing and songs, in a state of near hypnotic trance, until the dancers dropped from exhaustion in a true faint. While under the spell of the trance or faint, they experienced the visions and revelations promised. Part of the Sioux ritual was the wearing of specially prepared holy shirts and dresses, decorated with sacred symbols. The ceremonial dance shirt always had eagle feathers attached to the sleeves and shoulders. It was firmly believed

71

that the bullets of the enemy could not penetrate the shirt, thus the warriors were protected in battle. An eagle feather was also worn on the head. The cult spread rapidly among the reservations and the whites grew more apprehensive of the "new power" of the Indians. Alarm increased over the alleged possibility of new Indian outbreaks. Troops were called back to the area to keep the Indians in check. At the same time several Ghost Dance cult bands left the reservations. This led to the ultimate tragedy in December, 1890, of the Wounded Knee massacre. Chief Big Foot was intercepted by troops of the 7th Cavalry who surrounded the band and demanded that the Indians surrender their weapons. Only two rifles were produced; the soldiers began to search for more and a rifle shot apparently triggered the resultant chaotic massacre. Whatever the misunderstandings that may have caused the tragedy, it ended the Indians' armed opposition to the white man entering their land.

Most of the problems that plague the Sioux today have resulted from basic misunderstandings between the two cultures and the manner by which our government has attempted to minister to their needs. These people are first or second generation descendants of those hunters of the plains who were first forced onto the reservations and who saw their means of subsistence swept away and their social and cultural heritage crumble. They have continually struggled under suppression and through the trauma of forced change, in the attempt to adapt to the ways of the white man and at the same time retain at least a semblance of their once proud traditions and culture. They have experienced a particularly difficult transition to the concept of self-determination. Frustration, bitterness and anxiety have emerged as the natural result of this struggle. Acceptance of a different, frequently hostile, culture has not been easy. However, many local reservation communities are implementing social and educational programming utilizing their traditional culture and language. Tribal governing bodies, coupled with an increasing number of tribal members entering the professions, are making progress in the areas of health, employment, education and housing. Although it has taken a long time, progress has been made and, hopefully, will continue to be made. With new economic bases such as small industries on the reservations, revival of major interest in their culture and traditions, (both on their part and among whites), the construction of arts and crafts centers, etc., ways will be found which will bring about further understanding between Indian and white persons, and the ultimate solutions to the many problems that plague them.

Frank Fool's Crow, Ceremonial Chief of the Teton Sioux at Bear Butte in 1975. Photo courtesy Thomas E. Mails.

During the past thirty years the proportion of Indians to whites, considering the total population of South Dakota, has grown steadily. In the 1940's and 1950's the Indian population constituted 3.4% of the total; in 1960 it had increased to 3.7% and by 1970 was up to 6%.* Although not a large percentage, Indians do constitute a sizable group. The Sioux are aware of the influence they have had, and will have, on the life and history of this area. For futher information, see appendices A (Dakota Indian Reservations and Populations) and B (Sioux Religion, Culture and Traditions) on pp. 163 and 165.

*NOTE: By 1977 it was approximately 7%, and in 1989 it is approximately 9%.

74

Part III

BIOLOGICAL INFORMATION

BOTANICAL EXPLORATIONS AND INVESTIGATIONS
VEGETATION OF THE BLACK HILLS
ROCKY MOUNTAIN CONIFEROUS FOREST COMPLEX
NORTHERN CONIFEROUS FOREST COMPLEX
DECIDUOUS COMPLEX
GRASSLANDS COMPLEX
AMPHIBIANS AND REPTILES OF THE BLACK HILLS
MAMMALS OF THE BLACK HILLS
BIRDS OF THE BLACK HILLS

"The Black Hills, as I said, are very old mountains. More youthful ranges, such as the Alps and the Himalayas, show wide expanses of nudity, in the fashion of young people on the beach; but the Hills, in their green and vigorous old age, have become conservative and are clothed from neck to ankle—in ponderosa pine. Ponderosa, perhaps catching the habit from some of the scalawags of the early days, have had several aliases— rock pine, bull pine, western yellow pine—but ponderosa is their right name, according to the scientific folk who should know. And they make a beautiful garment. Whether they form the straight red pillars of a forest with centuries of maturity behind it or thickets of thirty-year-old saplings, whether they are climbing up a mountainside or marching down one, the ponderosa never lack charm. Individualists all, they vary much in form, and the eccentrics among them seem to pick out the most impossibly rocky spots for their homes and to grow there triumphantly, while the human onlooker wonders just what they have for nourishment, save air. They go clear up to the high, broken horizons and hobnob with the blue Black Hills sky, and in the night they loom higher and seem companions of the stars."

Quotation from Badger Clark, the legendary South Dakota poet, in his chapter in Roderick Peattie's *The Black Hills,* 1952. Vanguard Press, Inc., New York. pp. 22-23.

77

INTRODUCTION

The Black Hills area is in many respects one of the most fascinating in North America from the biological, particularly biogeographic and taxonomic, standpoints. Several factors have contributed toward making the Hills unique biologically. The climatic variability; their geographic location, near the center of the continent; their isolation as a mountainous upthrust surrounded on all sides by the High Plains; and variable topography, have combined in this relatively restricted area to produce an extremely interesting and diverse flora and fauna. Here several biomes meet and overlap . . . a Cordilleran element, the Great Plains element, the Northern Coniferous element, and the eastern Deciduous Forest element. This overlapping of ranges of organisms belonging to several different geographic elements has resulted in the creation of a "whirlpool effect" of distributions involving many taxonomic groups, both plant and animal.

The area, therefore, offers the biologist a unique opportunity for study. Many western forms reach the eastern limit of their range here and overlap with the westernmost extension of eastern forms. Likewise many northern species reach the southern limit of their range here and overlap with central Great Plains forms. In some cases a resultant hybridization of distinctive taxa has occurred, adding to the potential interest. The area affords a readily accessible, relatively small region where one can encounter and study representatives of these diverse geographic elements, plus a number of hybrid forms, without traveling great distances.

There is evidence that this sort of overlap was once more widespread, extending to the south along the east slope of the Rocky Mountains, but now occurs principally in the Black Hills. Thus, the Hills area remains as an important, unique, "outdoor laboratory" for the biologist.

BOTANICAL EXPLORATIONS AND INVESTIGATIONS

Although most of the early explorations of the Black Hills were organized for other purposes, and cannot honestly be classified as botanical in nature, many of the parties included men who made scientific and technical observations and collections and prepared lists of the flora of the area. A chronological list and brief description of plant collections that were made, either as part of geological or military explorations or those organized strictly for floral study, are presented here.

Date of Exploration or Collection	Summary Account
1823	Probably the first record of a botanical nature was that reported by James Clyman with the Jedediah Smith party. Clyman describes a "grove of petrified timber . . . some of the trees so large . . . I couldn't reach around the trunk. . . ."
1857	The next record of note was the report, published in 1862, of the Lt. Warren-Dr. Hayden expedition. The party collected and listed 700 species of plants from the area, with 32 reported from the Black Hills, identified by Dr. George Englemann.
1874	The Custer expedition report, published by Ludlow in 1875, includes the lists of plants collected in the Black Hills. Professor H. B. Donaldson collected 75 species, belonging to 55 genera and 23 plant families . . . all identified by Professor John Coulter. In addition N. H. Winchell (the geologist) collected and identified 36 trees and shrubs.
1875	The final report (1880) of the Newton-Jenney expedition included a listing of 166 seed plants and 9 "fernworts" all identified by Asa Gray.
1892	The first serious scientific study of the plants

of the region was undertaken by Per Axel Rydberg, for the United States Department of Agriculture. Finally published in 1896, his *Flora of the Black Hills of South Dakota* includes 700 species of vascular plants plus much taxonomic and ecological data.

1895   T. A. Williams published a list of native trees and shrubs of South Dakota, including Black Hills species.

1898   Charles E. Bessey collected in the Hills and published a short paper.

1899   D. A. Saunders published his *Ferns and Flowering Plants of South Dakota* that includes several hundred plants from the Black Hills. This publication was based largely on Rydberg's collections.

From 1900 on there have been many botanical investigations and publications. Notable among them are the work of S. D. Visher (1908, 1911, 1912), C. R. Ball (1908, 1910, 1913), John Murdock (1908-1912), A. S. Hitchcock (1914), W. P. Carr (1914), E. H . Hayward (1926-27), and E. J. Palmer (1929).

Special mention should be made of several very important additions to the floral literature of the Black Hills. Prof. Wm. H. Over's *Trees and Shrubs of South Dakota* (1923) and his later *Flora of South Dakota* (1932) both contain important material on the Black Hills. Another significant contribution is that of Arthur C. McIntosh, *A Botanical Survey of the Black Hills of South Dakota* (1931). This work has to be considered as one of the most inclusive publications on Black Hills flora. In more recent years (1959) John M. & Clara K. Winter and Theodore Van Bruggen released their *Check List of the Vascular Plants of South Dakota*. Van Bruggen's *Vascular Plants of South Dakota* was published in 1976. This is the most definitive work on the flora of the state.

There are countless other Black Hills floral publications, far too numerous to mention here, most of which are specialized and restricted to a particular taxon, or are practically oriented. They are of limited use to the general reader.

80

Black Fox Canyon, burned in 1939. Photo by author, 1971.

VEGETATION OF THE BLACK HILLS

There are four rather distinct vegetative complexes that characterize the Black Hills: (1) a Rocky Mountain Coniferous Forest complex dominated by ponderosa pine (*Pinus ponderosa* Laws.), (2) a Northern Coniferous Forest Complex consisting of white spruce (*Picea glauca* [Moench] Voss) and associated species, (3) the Grassland Complex of the northern Great Plains, (4) a Deciduous Forest Complex, primarily eastern, occurring in shaded north-and-east-slope situations and along drainages at lower elevations and progressing upstream from the adjacent Plains. A major component of the deciduous complex, considered by some investigators as a separate fifth complex, is a Mixed Shrub element.

Hayward (1928), and MacIntosh (1931), both studied the percentage, origin and composition of more than 1000 species of plants in the Black Hills. Their studies reveal that 30% were Rocky Mountain species; 17% were Great Plains species; 9% were eastern deciduous forms; 6% were northern; 4.5% were

81

southwestern; with the remainder representing widespread species plus introduced forms and others. It is interesting to note that only .5% were considered as possible endemics. Such investigations reinforce the position that the Black Hills is truly an area of vegetational diversity.

.ROCKY MOUNTAIN CONIFEROUS FOREST COMPLEX

The ponderosa pine forest constitutes the largest single element in the Black Hills. This dominant forest, covering the majority of the forested area, is obviously the type that characterizes the Hills and gives them their name. There are still areas, although they are becoming increasingly rare, where the ponderosa pine is the only tree type present.*

A past history of frequent and sometimes extensive fires, cutting and clearing for timber, mining, grazing and seed crops,

Ponderosa Pine thinning operation. Photo by author, 1989.

*Note: Local natives, particularly those who have worked in the lumber mills, frequently refer to varieties of pine they claim occur in the Hills using such names as yellow pine, bull pine, rock pine and others. These are undoubtedly local varieties of the ponderosa. This particular pine exhibits a great deal of morphological variation throughout its range, and it is not strange that different names have been applied locally.

82

all have taken their toll so that very few undisturbed areas remain. There are restricted areas where relatively large stands of dog-haired pine (crowded, stunted clusters of small trees) still occur. However, an intensive program of leasing such timber for "post and pole" cutting has become an increasingly common practice in recent years. As a result, most of the Hills have been selectively thinned by this program. Since such thinning and clearing practices have been going on for many years the trees that remain have grown more rapidly and are much larger in average size. Records indicate that the largest pine trees that presently occur in the Hills are approximately 24 inches in diameter representing an average maximum age of about 160 years.

Ponderosa pine is very tolerant of dry, hot growing conditions. It thrives on rocky soil, roots deeply by developing a long taproot that grows down into fractured rock relatively easily. It does not grow well in clay, but thrives on the Minnekahta limestone and sandstone type of soil.

The ridges and hills at higher elevations are typically covered with pine, with the lower valleys, draws, and lowlands exhibiting the grasslands complex. In the foothills, the ecotone between the grasslands complex and the pine forest presents a rather irregular borderline, generally occurring at approximately the 4000 ft. mark. The overall effect is that of picturesque fingerlike projections of pine forest extending down into the valleys and foothills from the more solidly forested higher elevations. This pattern, coupled with the invasion of the deciduous element along drainages, presents the interesting mixture of the three major vegetation complexes.

In more open pine forest situations an understory of common ground juniper (*Juniperus communis* L.) and, or, kinnikinnik or bearberry (*Arctostaphylos uva-ursi* [L.] Spreng.) characteristically occurs. The kinnikinnik takes the typical form of an extensive ground cover. The ground juniper varies from isolated individuals to large thickets. Creeping cedar (*Juniperus horizontalis* Moench.) also occurs locally and forms heavy thickets.

In open disturbed areas and on the forest edge, the quaking aspen (*Populus tremuloides* Michx.) commonly occurs. Locally,

83

Aspen and Ponderosa Pine on the Limestone Plateau. Photo by author, 1972.

particularly in old burn areas, aspen stands are very extensive. Large areas, in the northern Hills especially, are dominated by aspen forests although the more typical pattern throughout the Hills is a borderline forest, or mixed stands among the pine forest.

The poorly lighted and relatively dry soil immediately beneath pine stands is often devoid of herbaceous vegetation. However, where openings in the coniferous canopy are present and moisture is more abundant, lush flowering plant displays are frequently encountered throughout the growing season. A definite succession of such floral displays occurs as the season progresses. Indeed, the same area may appear to be entirely different, so far as the flowering plant species are concerned, at one time in comparison to several weeks later.

Another major coniferous tree, the western red cedar, or Rocky Mountain cedar, (*Juniperus scopulorum* Sarg.), forms "woodlands" in the southwest and southern hills and extends to the east of the Hills in breaks and draws, following the ridges as far as the Missouri River. Associated with this drier habitat type are currant (*Ribes* spp.), mountain mahogany (*Cercocarpus montanus* Raf.), and sumac (*Rhus* spp.).

84

There are two additional species of pine that occur in isolated stands in the Black Hills. The lodgepole pine (*Pinus contorta* [Dougl.]) occurs in a sparsely distributed stand covering a total

Lodgepole Pine near Nahant. Photo by author, 1972.

area of approximately 150 acres in the Nahant Area. There have been reports that it occurs in small patches elsewhere; however, these reports have been carefully checked, and it is doubtful that there are other localities where it is found. The Nahant site does have several pockets separated from one another, but they are all in the same general locality. They occur at an elevation of approximately 6000 ft. along Buskala Creek about two miles northwest of Nahant, Lawrence County, South Dakota, in sections 20, 28 and 29 of T3N, R3E. They are more common on the south side of the creek than on the north, and they extend up the slopes to the ridge tops. The nearest locations where Lodgepole pine occurs naturally are in the Bighorn Mountains of Wyoming, over 150 miles west of the Black Hills, and in the Laramie Range at about the same distance to the southwest, also in Wyoming. The other species, the limber pine (*Pinus flexilis* James) is found as a small stand in the Cathedral spires area near Harney Peak and very close to the Pennington-Custer County line. The altitude of this stand is 6600-6800 ft. The nearest locations for other limber pine forests are in the Bighorn Mountains and a restricted stand in the Little Missouri Badlands of North Dakota. There is also an area in southwestern Nebraska where they occur as an isolated stand.

On the basis of evidence from borings and ring counts of both the lodgepole and limber pine, it would appear that they have been in the Black Hills for over 200 years. This means that they were here long before the white man. Thus, both species pose interesting distributional problems. How did they get here; were they introduced by the Indians or are they representative relicts of a once larger forest? Some investigators have postulated the theory that they were once more widely distributed in the area, and this must be considered as one explanation for their occurrence here. For futher information on these stands, see D. J. Rogers' paper.*

NORTHERN CONIFEROUS FOREST COMPLEX

In addition to the dominant pine forest the second major conifer, the white spruce (*Picea glauca* [Moench] Voss), occurs commonly in the Black Hills. A Northern Coniferous forest species, the spruce reaches its southern limit in the Hills. Its occurrence here represents an isolated pocket separated from its continuous range to the north by several hundred miles. It forms locally dense forests at suitable habitats in the northern Hills and extends as far south as the Custer State Park area and the Harney range where relatively extensive stands occur at higher

---

*Rogers, D. J. 1969. *Isolated Stands of Lodgepole Pine and Limber Pine in the Black Hills.* Proc. S.D. Acad. Sci. Vol. 48:138-147.

White Spruce; a north facing slope exposure.
Photo by author.

elevations in cool canyons. Typically it is found on the north slopes and in moist situations. There are some areas that support a particularly lush spruce forest, such as the Limestone area, Black Fox Canyon, and the headwaters of Spearfish Canyon. The lower branches of the spruce are invariably draped with old man's beard (*Usnea cavernosa* Fr.), the lichen that occupies an ecological niche similar to spanish moss. The understory in these stands resembles that of a typical northern dense forest, with lush fern, moss, lichen, sedge and grass communities plus many flowering plant species. Such exotics as the yellow lady's slipper (*Cypripedium calceolus* L.), green-flowered orchid (*Habenaria saccata* Greene), the bracted orchid (*Habenaria viridis* [L.] R. Br.) and the fairy or Venus' slipper (*Calypso bulbosa* [L.] Oakes) occur here, although they are rare. The yellow lady's slipper and the fairy slipper are among the rarest flow-

87

ers that occur in the Black Hills. On the edges of clearings are found such shrubs as the red-elderberry (*Sambucus racemosa* L.), nannyberry (*Viburnum lentago* L.), grouseberry (*Vaccinium scoparium* Leiberg) and serviceberry (*Amelanchier alnifolia* Nutt.). In more moist, cool and shaded areas the paper birch (*Betula papyrifera* Marsh.) flourishes.

DECIDUOUS COMPLEX

The most extensive deciduous complex occurs along drainages at lower elevations, progressing upstream from the adjacent plains. In these situations the complex consists primarily of a mixture of bur oak (*Quercus macrocarpa* Michx.), American elm (*Ulmus americana* L.), green ash (*Fraxinus pennsylvanica* Marsh.), box elder (*Acer negundo* L.) and eastern hop-hornbeam (*Ostrya virginiana* [Mill.] K. Koch). As would be expected, in the Plains and in the lower foothills the cottonwood (*Populus deltoides* Marsh.) and the peach-leaved willow (*Salix amygdaloides* Anderss.) are the dominant streamside trees but become less frequent at the point where the streams emerge from the Hills proper. At these locations the deciduous element rather abruptly becomes the more typically mixed type. As the elevation increases, most of the species disappear and quaking aspen (*Populus tremuloides* Michx.) and paperbirch (*Betula papyrifera* Marsh.) become dominant deciduous forms. Also becoming more pronounced is a dense shrub complex consisting of various willow species (*Salix* spp.), river birch (*Betula occidentalis* Hook.), red osier dogwood (*Cornus stolonifera* Michx.) and other shrubby types.

The northern Hills support a more widespread deciduous forest than the southern Hills because of increased moisture, cooler temperature and exposure factors. The extreme northern slope of the Hills, especially, supports a relatively dense deciduous forest with bur oak the dominant species. The areas to the north of Deadwood and southwest of Spearfish are well-covered with oak, which seems to be the only species able to establish itself some distance away from streams, particularly at lower

88

elevations. At the lower edge of the foothills the oak is more "scrubby" with the trees getting larger as the altitude increases. Toward the upper portions of the north slope, particularly in the Limestone area, a more lush, typical mixed forest emerges with paper birch becoming dominant. This north slope area may represent an extensive old burn with the oak establishing itself, replacing the pine. It would be conjecture to speculate as to whether or not a pine forest will ultimately replace the oak. At this point, it seems unlikely since the oak is so well established and would appear to be the "climax forest" in these restricted areas. The herbaceous understory of the foothills canyons includes a wide variety of northern and eastern flowering types.

The shrub component of the deciduous complex is considered by some investigators to be extensive enough to warrant consideration as a separate, fourth complex. However, it is primarily deciduous in nature, occurs in the same situations, and thus will be considered here as a part of the larger deciduous complex. There are both eastern and western species among the shrubs and, in different localities, the dominants vary a great deal, actually forming specific communities.

In relatively undisturbed areas at medium to high elevations, and occurring as streamside and floodplain communities throughout the major portion of the Hills, is a dense shrub zone consisting of a mixture of several willow species, particularly *Salix bebbiana* Sarg., *Salix lutea* Nutt., *Salix interior* Rowlee (other willow species occur locally including *S. planifolia* Pursh., *S. discolor* Muhl. and *S. petiolaris* J. E. Smith), riverbirch (*Betula occidentalis* Hook.), red osier dogwood (*Cornus stolonifera* Michx.), wild rose (*Rosa* spp.), raspberry (*Rubus* spp.) and currant (*Ribes* spp.). Unfortunately most riparian (moist, streamside) habitats have been badly disturbed by clearing, burning and spraying for grazing or agricultural purposes so that very little of the once-lush floodplain vegetation remains. Most of the willows are in generally poor condition with many species almost decimated. In many areas dead or dying individuals are more common than living ones. The result is that many valleys, particularly the broad, parklike areas of the higher hills, exhibit open grassland up to the stream's edge. No shrub zone

89

persists. A notable exception is the Rapid Creek area east of Rochford. A comparison of this relatively undisturbed lush floodplain vegetation with that of most other drainages presents a stark contrast.

A general lowering of the water table has also contributed to the near decimation of a once heavy shrub zone along most of the streams. The typical pattern has been that the grass-sedge-forb communities have become established and the woody types driven out.

Even in the open meadows at medium to high elevations, where a definite tall shrub zone once occurred, consisting primarily of Bebb's willow (*Salix bebbiana* Sarg.) between the pine forest and the grasslands, today there is an abrupt line of demarcation between the forest and grassland. Quaking aspen (*Populus tremuloides* Michx.) stands do occur on the borderline in many situations. However the typical pattern is one of pine-grasslands. This is particularly true in the Limestone plateau and throughout the Central and Southern Hills.

Another dominant shrub community occurring throughout the central hills both along floodplains of drainages and in open meadows is the snowberry or wolfberry (*Symphoricarpos occidentalis* Hook.). Locally it forms a dense thicketlike cover from a foot to perhaps three feet in height. In the west central hills at higher elevations shrubby cinquefoil (*Potentilla fruticosa* L.) is locally abundant, forming a shrub zone between the forest and grasses.

At higher elevations in the Northern Hills the mountain balm or "deerbrush" (*Ceanothus velutinus* Dougl.) occurs in disturbed areas, particularly old forest burns. Locally heavy stands occur in the Terry Peak area. *Ceanothus fendleri* A. Gray also occurs locally in the limestone area.

One of the major shrub communities, occurring along the western edge of the Black Hills and extending south and east is the mountain mahogany (*Cercocarpus montanus* Raf.) community. In lower, drier situations mountain mahogany exhibits a characteristic open distribution. The individual shrubs are relatively small (4 ft.), but at higher, more moist, locations individuals exceed 10 ft. in height and form dense thickets. Normally it

90

is confined to soil containing calcareous parent materials. Typically associated with the mountain mahogany are currant (*Ribes* spp.), sumac (*Rhus trilobata* Nutt.) and western red cedar (*Juniperus scopulorum* Sarg.).

In the lower foothills, particularly in the north, the buffaloberry (*Shepherdia canadensis* [L.] Nutt.) occurs in locally heavy populations in depressions or slightly sheltered areas. These stands may be relatively monospecific or they must occur in association with coral berry or sumac.

The conspicuous sagebrush association occupies extensive areas of lowlands in all directions from the Hills, although it is particularly well-developed to the south and southwest. The dominant species is common sagebrush (*Artemisia tridentata* Nutt.). This species usually indicates a dry, fertile, non-saline type of soil. On sandier soil the smaller sandsage (*Artemisia filifolia* Torr.) typically dominates. The tall rabbit brush (*Chrysothamnus nauseosus* [Pall.] Britt.) is especially abundant on eroded soil along ravines. With sufficient rainfall the mixed prairie grasses compete favorably with the sage.

Coyote. Photo courtesy Kent Fish, 1976.

91

GRASSLANDS COMPLEX

The Great Plains grassland complex forms the dominant vegetation surrounding the Black Hills and extending for some distance in every direction from them. Obviously this is the setting that has led to the designation of the Hills as a "forested island in a grassland sea." Depending upon local moisture and soil conditions, the complex typically consists of a high Plains and foothills mixture of grasses, forbs and some low shrub types that reflect elements of true shortgrass prairie, midgrass prairie and bunchgrass types. The dominant grasses include western wheatgrass (*Agropyron smithii* Rydb.), needle and thread (*Stipa comata* Trin. and Rupr.), green needlegrass (*Stipa viridula* Trin.), prairie junegrass (*Koeleria pyramidata* [Lam.] Beauv.), blue grama (*Bouteloua gracilis* [H.B.K.] Griffiths), side-oats grama (*Bouteloua curtipendula* [Michx.] Torr.) and buffalo grass (*Buchloe dactyloides* [Nutt.] Engelm.). Japanese chess (*Bromus japonicus* Thunb.) and cheat grass (*Bromus tectorum* L.), two introduced species, are commonly found. Also found are little bluestem (*Andropogon scoparius* Michx.), prairie cordgrass (*Spartina pectinata* Link.) and prairie dropseed (*Sporobolus heterolepis* A. Gray), plus many other native and introduced species.

Typical forbs include prickly pear, (*Opuntia* spp.), yucca (*Yucca glauca* Nutt.), prairie clovers (*Petalostemon* spp.), American vetch (*Vicia americana* Muhl.), lead plant (*Amorpha canescens* Pursh.), many composites (*e.g., Helianthus* spp.,

Sharp-tailed Grouse "dancing". Photo courtesy B. J. Rose.

92

Erigeron spp., *Aster* spp.), purple cone-flower (*Echinacea angustifolia* DC) and scores of others.

To the north of the Black Hills, western wheatgrass and Montana wheatgrass (*Agropyron dasystachyum* [Hook.] Scribn. and Smith) are the major types with scattered distributions of blue grama and buffalo grass. Needle and thread is abundant locally in lighter soils. Buffalo grass and blue grama achieve their greatest abundance in the areas south and east of the Hills. The sandy soils to the southeast and southwest support locally abundant stands of big bluestem (*Andropogon gerardi* Vitman), prairie sandreed (*Calamovilfa longifolia* [Hook.] Scribn.), and Indian ricegrass (*Oryzopsis hymenoides* [Roem, and Schult.] Ricker).

On rangelands that are in good condition in the Badlands region, western wheatgrass and blue grama are dominant, with a mixture of other grasses also present. If conditions are bad, typically the result of overgrazing and, or, drought, the short grasses and sedges become abundant. There are many introduced species that appear to do very well in the Black Hills area. In addition native grasses are cultivated for livestock purposes.

Reynolds Prairie. Photo courtesy Robert Evenson, 1977.

93

Characteristic of the Black Hills proper are large, open, park-like valleys, prairies and meadows which consist of grasslands supporting a wide variety of grasses and forbs. These typically occur at higher elevations and are of varying size. Two of the largest are Reynolds prairie and Gillette prairie in the Central Hills west of Deerfield, each of which covers several square miles. Danby Park in the southern Hills, west of Custer, is approximately 3 miles long and ½ to 1 mile wide. In the Northern Hills these open areas are numerous and are usually irregular in shape and size. The Limestone area, where they are more meadow-like in nature, exhibits the largest concentration of them.

One of the most interesting features of these areas is the abrupt transition between the pine or spruce forest and the open grassland. As discussed earlier under the section on shrubs, there is a noticeable lack of a shrub zone. The question as to what have been the causes for the formation of these "high prairies" remains somewhat a mystery. There have been many explanations postulated in the attempt to explain them: (1) Some investigators think they were established by severe fires and are thus old burn areas that have been maintained by the inability of the trees to become established in a quickly-formed, well-established grass sod, (2) others feel that they may represent old erosion surface, and/or (3) there is a gravel subsoil with a washed-in topsoil that affords a good soil base for sod but not for trees, with the result that competition drives the trees out. No doubt the soil plays a dominant role in the peculiar, interesting distribution. Whatever the cause, the result is a very picturesque landscape effect with the forest background and grassland foreground representing two distinctive floral complexes.

In the Northern and Central Hills the higher meadows exhibit a dominant association that includes these grasses: Kentucky bluegrass (*Poa pratensis* L.), timothy (*Phleum pratense* L.), brome (*Bromus* spp.), needlegrass (*Stipa* spp.), wheatgrass (*Agropyron* spp.), and wild rye (*Elymus* spp.). The forbs present a striking display seasonally and include such species as: wood lily (*Lilium philadelphicum* L.), beard-tongue or "snapdragon"

94

(*Penstemon* spp.), fleabane (*Erigeron* spp.), wild bergamot (*Monarda fistulosa* L.), Aster (*Aster* spp.) sego lily (*Calochortus gunnisonii* S. Wats.), Indian paintbrush (*Castilleja sessiliflora* Pursh.), goldenrod (*Solidago* spp.), black-eyed Susan (*Rudbeckia hirta* L.), sunflower (*Helianthus* spp.), false dandelion (*Agoseris glauca* [Pursh.] D. Dietr.), and bastard toadflax (*Comandra umbellata* [L.] Nott.).

In the drier parts of the Southern Hills grasslands, and in exposed rocky southfacing slopes at lower elevations in the Central area, the following representative species are found: little bluestem (*Andropogon scoparius* Michx.), blue grama (*Bouteloua gracilis* [H.B.K.] Griffiths), buffalo grass (*Buchloe dactyloides* [Nutt.] Engelm.), Japanese chess (*Bromus japonicus* Thunb.), prickly pear (*Opuntia* spp.), yucca (*Yucca glauca* Nutt.), pasture sage (*Artemisia frigida* Willd.), and mountain lily (*Leucocrinum montanum* Nutt.). In more moist situations Western wheatgrass (*Agropyron smithii* Rydb.) and prairie junegrass (*Koeleria pyramidata* [Lam.] Beauv.) are locally abundant.

Another distinctive type of community occurs in wet meadows, near streams and beaver dams. In these situations several species of sedge, including *Carex aurea* Nutt., and *Carex rostrata* Stokes, are dominant. In better drained areas sedgegrass meadows are common. In these localities grasses such as tufted hairgrass (*Deschampsia caespitosa* [L.] Beauv.) and northern reedgrass (*Calamagrostis inexpansa* A. Gray) are found, along with many sedges (*Carex* spp.). In these moist meadows lush flowering plant displays occur seasonally. For example, large areas frequently appear to be completely covered by blue larkspur (*Delphinium nuttalianum* Pritz) in the spring, blue flag or Rocky Mountain iris (*Iris missouriensis* Nutt.) in early summer, yarrow (*Achillea millefolium* L.) and wild bergamot (*Monarda fistulosa* L.) in mid-summer, and asters (*Aster* spp.) and sunflowers (*Helianthus* spp.) in late summer. Many other species, too numerous to mention, are present in large quantities and contribute to the constantly changing effect of the floral displays. Obviously the extent and duration of the bloom is dependent on temperature and moisture conditions and varies from year to year. To the casual observer, such an abundance of flowers would seem to indicate that they were actually cultivated. In a typical year these floral displays follow a characteristic seasonal calendar, beginning in the southern hills and steadily progressing northward as the season advances.

AMPHIBIANS AND REPTILES OF THE BLACK HILLS

The Black Hills present a total ecological complex that is not very well suited to a highly developed, representative herpetological fauna. This is largely due to the relatively high altitude and temperate climate, in addition to the relative isolation of the upthrust in the middle of a high dry Plains. The isolated location undoubtedly presents an obstacle to migration or perhaps even survival of a slow, highly specialized type of animal. Amphibians and reptiles are also probably more climate-dependent or restricted than other animals and are in general not very well adapted to mountainous, temperate conditions. Such factors as: the wide range in temperature extremes, particularly the low winter temperatures resulting in a low frost line; low humidity; generally low rainfall; normally hot days and cool nights during the summer, late spring and early fall seasons; and frequent summer hailstorms, all undoubtedly contribute to a relatively hostile environment for amphibians and reptiles.

Although the Black Hills and surrounding area are generally regarded as semi-arid, there are several moderately sized artificial reservoirs and lakes in the Hills proper and in the surrounding Plains. In addition there are numerous beaver dams, stock dams and streams present. These localities present suitable habitat, although very restricted, for several types of animals that require an aquatic or semi-aquatic habitat. Thus, the amphibians, turtles and a number of snake species inhabit these areas, resulting in local distributions for them. Environmental conditions that are conducive to large reptile populations, such as uniformly warm temperatures, relatively high humidity and high insect populations as a food base, simply do not exist in the Black Hills.

The overall result is that in the Black Hills there are proportionately fewer species among the "herps" than among the other major animal groups. Based on authenic records and reports of competent herpetologists, the number of recorded species present in the Hills totals 22, including 7 amphibian and 15 reptile species (although there is some difference of opinion as to which subspecies are present). In the following checklist and in

97

those cited, ordinarily if a species is reported it means a sight record of a competent observer, whereas an official record means that a specimen has been collected, preserved and is on deposit in the collection of a college or university or private institution, thus being available for authentication by any interested party.

Three of the investigators who have made extensive studies and collections of the amphibians and reptiles of the Black Hills are: (1) Mr. Earl Chace, the well-known herpetologist, affiliated with the Black Hills Reptile Gardens near Rapid City; Mr. Chace specializes in reptiles. He published a paper and checklist, *The Reptiles of Paha Sapa,* in *Animal Kingdom,* a popular periodical in August 1971, in which he reported 14 species of reptiles as occurring in the Black Hills. (2) Dr. Hobart M. Smith, a professional biologist from the University of Colorado, Boulder, prepared an unpublished, mimeographed *Checklist of Amphibians and Reptiles Known from the Black Hills of South Dakota and Wyoming,* 1964. Dr. Smith also reports 14 species of reptiles but differs from Chase on 4 species. In addition Smith includes 7 species of amphibians. (3) Mr. Charles Peterson, currently working on his doctorate at Washington State University, did his master's degree thesis (University of Illinois, 1975) on the amphibians and reptiles of the Black Hills. Peterson collected in the Hills extensively over a two year period, and, as a result, has compiled the most accurate checklist of amphibians and reptiles, based on documented collections, from this area. Peterson lists 7 species of amphibians and 15 species of reptiles as definitely occurring in the Black Hills. In addition he indicates that one lizard subspecies may occur in the southeastern portion, (*Sceloporus undulatus*). Included in the 22 total species are 1 salamander, 3 toads, 3 frogs, 3 turtles, 2 lizards and 10 snakes. Other investigators have reported two additional forms, the mudpuppy (*Necturus maculosus*) and the ribbon garter snake (*Thamnophis proximus*), as being present in the Hills. However, their status is questionable, not having been recorded officially.

The following checklist includes all species of amphibians and reptiles that have been reported from the Black Hills. The list

98

includes the authority, based on the collections and checklists of the three investigators named above and coded as C = Chace, P = Peterson and S = Smith. A brief statement on general abundance and distribution is included, largely taken, or modified, from Peterson's field notes.

AMPHIBIANS AND REPTILES OF THE BLACK HILLS

CLASS *AMPHIBIA*
Order *Caudata*—Salamanders

Common name	Scientific name	Investigator
1. Barred and/or Blotched Tiger Salamander	*Ambystoma tigrinum mavortium* Baird and/or *melanostictum*	S, P

Common, ranging throughout the Hills, from the Plains to as high as the Crooks tower region (7000+ ft.).

Order *Anura*—Frogs and Toads

2. Plains Spadefoot	*Scaphiopus bombifrons* Cope	S, P

Occurs in Plains, restricted to lower foothills. Peterson reports, "Recorded from Weston, (Wyo.), Fall River, Custer, Pennington and Meade Counties, but almost certainly occurring in the other counties as well. They inhabit grassland areas within the Black Hills (Red Valley, Minnekahta Plains) and also the surrounding plains. They are nocturnal in addition to spending much of their time burrowed into the ground, so are infrequently seen."

3. Great Plains Toad	*Bufo cognatus* Say	S, P

Occurs commonly in Plains, restricted to

99

foothills in Black Hills; Peterson lists six locality records, with a distribution similar to that of the Plains Spadefoot.

4. Rocky Mountain Toad or Common Western Toad — *Bufo woodhousii woodhousii* Girard — S, P

Occurs commonly in Plains, fairly common, and more widely distributed within the Hills than the other toad species, ranging into the Central Area from the lower foothills.

5. Boreal Chorus Frog — *Pseudacris triseriata maculata* Agassiz — S, P

Occurs commonly in Plains, and throughout the Hills, in either prairie or forested regions wherever suitable habitat is present (ponds, lakes, streams or marshy areas.) They can readily be heard chorusing in spring or early summer (as late as July at high elevations); after breeding more difficult to find.

6. Bullfrog — *Rana catesbeiana* Shaw — P

Peterson lists this species as occurring primarily in the southern Hills, locally abundant in the Hot Springs area; a few reports from lakes in the central Hills, but questionable.

7. Leopard Frog — *Rana pipiens pipiens* (Schreber) Pope — S, P

The *Rana pipiens* complex is a difficult one taxonomically. Dr. Donald Dunlap, Biology Department, U.S.D., considers the Black Hills form as the northern variety and assigns them to *Rana pipiens pipiens*. Occurs at all elevations in all counties of the Hills, extremely abundant.

100

CLASS *REPTILIA*

Order *Testudines*—Turtles

8. Western
Painted Turtle
Chrysemys picta belli (Gray)
Schmidt
C, S, P.

Fairly common in the Plains and possibly in the Hills. Recorded from Pennington and Custer Counties, with observations from several other points, including Meade County. Probably more common than records indicate.

9. Common Snap-
ping Turtle
Chelydra serpentina serpentina (L.) Pope
C

Common in the Plains and reported from several locations in the Hills. Collected in Custer State Park (Grace Coolidge Creek and two miles west of Mt. Coolidge), reported from Beaver Creek in Wind Cave National Park, and Spring Creek.

10. Western Spiny
Softshell Turtle
Trionyx spiniferus hartwegi Conant and Goin
C, P

Occurs in Plains, rare in Hills, reported from only one locality, Beaver Creek in the west central Hills, just across the state line in Weston County, Wyoming.

Order *Squamata*

Suborder *Sauria*—Lizards

11. Northern Sage-
brush Lizard
Sceloporus graciosus graciosus Baird and Girard
P

Rare in the Black Hills, recorded from only two localities: Thompson Canyon, southwest of Moon in the west central part; and six miles east of Moon, Pennington County. They probably occur in other localities, typically in dry areas, associated with western red cedar, mountain mahogany, yucca, etc.

101

12. Eastern Short   *Phrynosoma douglassii*   C, S, P
    Horned Lizard   *brevirostre* Girard

    Occurs in the surrounding Plains and in the
    Hills, probably restricted to northern and
    southern portions; not common, recorded
    from Fall River County, Meade County, burn
    areas near Moskee, (Wyo.), prefers dry
    "burnoffs."

                 Suborder *Serpentes*—Snakes

13. Black Hills   *Storeria occipitomaculata*   C, S, P
    Red-bellied   *pahasapae* Storer
    Snake

    Probably restricted to the Hills proper; Smith
    considers the Black Hills population as sub-
    specifically distinct. Peterson has recorded
    them from fifteen localities, all in the Central
    Area or the Limestone Plateau. Less com-
    mon than the green snake, but not rare; us-
    ually found under surface objects (logs,
    rocks, boards) in or near moist open areas in
    forested regions.

14. Western Wan-   *Thamnophis elegans vagrans*   C, S, P
    dering Garter   Baird and Girard
    Snake

    Restricted to the Black Hills in South Dakota,
    recorded from the Central Area and Lime-
    stone Plateau; common around streams but
    also in moist areas away from water. The
    Black Hills probably represents the eastern-
    most edge of its range.

15. Western Plains   *Thamnophis radix haydeni*   C, S, P
    Garter Snake   Kennicott

    Very common in the surrounding Plains, and
    occurs in the Hills; recorded from Meade,
    Pennington, and Custer Counties, probably

restricted to lower elevations; typical habitat is near ponds and moist grasslands.

16. Red-sided Garter Snake (Red-barred)   *Thamnophis sirtalis parietalis* Say   C, S, P

Probably the most common snake in the Black Hills, recorded from many areas; less frequent at higher elevations, prefers aquatic or moist habitat.

17. Western Hog-nose Snake   *Heterodon nasicus nasicus* Cagle   C, S, P

Primarily a Plains species, although not common; rare in the Black Hills proper, recorded specimens taken in the Red Valley. Considered to be primarily a nocturnal species, it is difficult to assess its frequency or occurrence.

18. Eastern Yellow-Bellied Racer   *Coluber constrictor flaviventris* Say   C, S, P

Moderately abundant in the surrounding Plains and in the Red Valley and Minnekahta Plains within the Hills; prefers open or semi-open habitat; probably does not extend into higher elevations.

19. Smooth Green Snake   *Opheodrys vernalis,* sub-species: *vernalis* Necker (Eastern) or *blanchardi* Grobman (Western) ?   C, S, P

The subspecific status of this species is unclear; Smith assigns the Black Hills form to the Eastern subspecies (*vernalis*); Peterson is inclined to assign it to the Western (*blanchardi*). In either event, the green snake is moderately common in the Hills, being most abundant in the Central Area and in the Limestone Plateau; in the Northern Hills it

103

occurs almost to the inner edge of the Red Valley. They are most frequently found in moist meadows in forested areas but may be encountered in drier conditions occasionally. They prefer to remain under boards, logs or other debris during the day but may be found along roads in early morning or late afternoon.

20. Bull Snake   *Pituophis melanoleucus sayi*   C, S, P
Schlegel

Essentially a Prairie and Plains species, moderately common in the surrounding areas and foothills to medium elevations in the Hills. Occurs in the Red Valley and Minnekahta Plains, extending for short to moderate distances into the Central Area.

21. Milk Snake   *Lampropeltis triangulum*   C
(Lacepede) Ditmars

Smith lists the subspecies *multistrata* and calls it the Northern Plains Red Kingsnake. Peterson uses the same subspecies, but calls it the Pallid, or Pale, Milk Snake. Chace lists a Western Milk Snake (*Lampropeltis triangulum gentilis* Baird and Girard). It is probably the same form, with few documented records upon which to base a judgement. Apparently relatively rare, although specimens have been collected in the Lead, Rapid City and Wind Cave areas, with observations in Spearfish, Hisega and Keystone. Primarily occurs in the Central Area forested regions.

22. Prairie Rattle-   *Crotalus viridis viridis*   C, S, P
snake   Rafinesque

Common throughout the surrounding Plains and in the foothills and lower elevations of the Black Hills; rarely occurring above 5000

104

ft., although there are records to indicate they have been collected at higher elevations. They inhabit a wide variety of habitats from grassland to streamside to rocky outcrops of ridges and hills. During dry, hot seasons they are moderately abundant at the lower elevations of the Hills proper. The prairie rattler is the only poisonous reptile in South Dakota.

POSSIBLE ADDITIONAL SPECIES

The following three species of "herps" have been reported, but not definitely recorded from the Hills.

Mudpuppy *Necturus maculosus* (Raf.) Eycleshymer

Rare, if present at all; reported by Smith from the Northern Hills (reportedly in the Deadwood-Lead area), not yet definitely recorded. Peterson states, "I do not believe it occurs in the Black Hills."

Rock Swift *Sceloporus undulatus* (Latreille) Garman

Smith lists it as S. *undulatus erythrocheilus;* not yet formally recorded, although "known to occur." Peterson states, "I have heard several second hand reports of a swift-like lizard occurring in the southeastern Hills. The habitat seems to be appropriate for *S. undulatus garmoni* (northern prairie lizard) and they are known to occur in counties east of the Hills."

Ribbon Garter Snake *Thamnophis proximus* Ditmars

Smith lists it as not yet formally recorded, although reliably observed; undoubtedly restricted to Hills proper. Chace does not list it; Peterson does not believe that it occurs in the Hills.

BIRDS OF THE BLACK HILLS

The Black Hills present a wide variety of habitats that provide the ornithologist with the opportunity to examine a diversity of ecologically different situations, most of which are extensive areas. Within a relatively short distance and time, the observer can visit the following habitats: Great Plains grassland; deciduous and coniferous woodlands or forests; mountains; fast- and slow-flowing streams; large, deep water reservoirs; and shallow water lakes, ponds, and stock or beaver dams with muddy shorelines. Largely because of such diversity the Black Hills have been relatively well-worked by ornithologists both on observational and collecting trips, particularly during recent years.

The greater majority of the birds in the Hills are western species, although there are eastern and northern forms that occur here. This fact, of itself, provides an interesting study opportunity. Because the Hills are located geographically in a fringe or borderline area between east and west, there is an overlap in range of eastern and western forms of closely allied taxons. This "geographic mixture" has resulted in hybridization of a number of varieties and offers an opportunity for the study of intergrades as well as parent types. (The Common Flicker, for example, is now regarded as a single species, with the Yellow-shafted and Red-shafted Flickers considered as races. The same situation occurs with the Baltimore and Bullock's Orioles, now identified as races of the Northern Oriole, because they regularly interbreed).

Many western species approach the eastern limit of their breeding ranges in the Hills. The White-winged Junco, Cassin's Finch, White-throated Swift, Lewis' Woodpecker, Poor-will, Western Wood Pewee, Western Flycatcher, Violet-green Swallow, Pinon Jay, Dipper, Mountain Bluebird, Townsend's Solitaire, Audubon's Warbler, and the colorful Western Tanager all nest here.

Eastern forms approaching the western limit of their breeding range include the Ovenbird and Indigo Bunting. There are many more "eastern" birds that occur here, but the majority of them extend their ranges beyond the Hills to the west.

The Northern Three-toed Woodpecker and the Black-backed Three-toed Woodpecker occur, although rarely, isolated by several hundred miles from their normal ranges.

Several boreal species nest here, including the Red-breasted Nuthatch, Gray Jay, Red Crossbill, Golden-crowned Kinglet, Solitary Vireo, and others. However, not many boreal or high mountain forms occur regularly, probably due to the lower elevation and isolation of the Hills. By the same token, few prairie species enter the Hills proper. It is interesting to note that, based on records of recent years, there appear to be increasing numbers of aquatic and shorebirds in the Hills. This is probably due to the relatively recent establishment of several major reservoirs which now have stabilized water levels. As with any region in the temperate zone bird populations fluctuate with the seasons with the winter populations relatively low. There is typically no major increase in populations during migratory seasons that would compare to other regions. Occasionally northern species will migrate in for short periods, probably as a result of adverse weather conditions and sparse food availability in their normal range.

One of the most striking observations the ornithologist will become aware of early in his field work in the Hills is that the pine forest supports a relatively sparse bird population. This fact presents an interesting problem. The reasons for low numbers are not known, but are well-documented by competent observers in the area. However, the number of species that inhabit the pine forest is still larger than that of other habitats, probably because of the large area covered by pine, and the intermixing of habitats.

A total of 139 individual species of birds occur regularly in the Black Hills, either remaining as permanent year-round residents or returning each year. Pettingill and Whitney list 131, differing on some species; the figure of 139 is based on recent records of observers in the area (Les Baylor, *et al*). An additional 87 species are occasional visitors, having been recorded at least once in modern times by a competent observer. There is only one endemic subspecies or race, the White-winged Junco (*Junco aikeni* R.) that occurs in the Hills. Actually there is even some question as to its endemic status since the A.O.U. checklist published in the AUK in April, 1973, (90:411-419), considers the White-winged, Slate-colored and Oregon Juncos as races of one species, the Dark-Eyed Junco. However, the White-winged Junco is distinguishable in the field. The Forest Service checklist identifies 24 species as rare or infrequent migrants, including such birds as the Common Loon, White Pelican, Wood Duck, Osprey, Blue Grosbeak and Clark's Nutcracker.

A complete checklist of the birds of the Black Hills can be found beginning on pg. 121. Although it is not possible to include descriptions and notes on the current status of all the birds that occur here, notes of general interest are included for twenty-five selected species. These were selected on the basis of personal experience and/or are those forms that typically attract much interest, question and comments from students and visitors to the Hills. The final list of twenty-five was compiled following consultation with several competent ornithologists familiar with Black Hills birds, including Prof. Les Baylor, Rapid City, Dr. Jack Saunders, Pierre, Dr. Robert Buckman, Madison, and Dr. Herbert Krause (deceased), Sioux Falls. Obviously, other birds could have been included or a different list could have been compiled—admittedly this is simply one list of many that would be possible to produce. Included are brief descriptions and notes on such factors as their current status, relative abundance, general distribution, preferred habitat or where one might reasonably expect to locate them in the field.

TWENTY-FIVE SELECTED BIRD SPECIES
IN THE BLACK HILLS

1. Turkey Vulture   *Cathartes aura* (Linnaeus)

   A large dark bird, soars in wide circles, holding wings in a broad V. A common carrion eater; a summer resident; occurs typically in more open areas at lower elevations, but can be found throughout the Hills; frequently mistaken for an eagle, except for the naked head and upturned wings; common to uncommon.

108

Red-Tailed Hawk. Photo courtesy Les Baylor.

2. Red-tailed Hawk   *Buteo jamaicensis* (Gmelin)

Common summer resident, but may occur throughout the year. Typically occurs in cliff or canyon areas near open meadows or burns. Nests in woodlands, feeds in open country. Often perches on poles or treetops—rarely hovers. The most frequently encountered hawk in the Hills, also the most easily identified by the uniformly colored tail, red above, lighter beneath, and a dark belly band.

3. Golden Eagle   *Aquila chrysaëtos* (Linnaeus)

A large, spectacular, dark brown bird with long, rounded wings usually seen soaring at high altitude. Permanent resident, occurring uncommonly to rare throughout the Hills, typically migrating to lower elevations or out onto the plains during the winter. Once numerous, numbers are declining, currently stringently protected. The eagles, both bald and golden, hold a special meaning for the Indians. Feathers once were used extensively by the Indians for decorative purposes and religious ceremonies. Possession of feathers now illegal . . . refer to the so-called "feather law."

4. Ruffed Grouse *Bonasa umbellus* (Linnaeus)

A fairly large, gray-brown, chicken-like bird, distinguished by the fan-like tail with a definite black terminal band. Although a permanent resident at all elevations, it is typically a fairly difficult bird to find; prefers deciduous woodlands or mixed forest; probably easier to locate in winter and spring. A northern or boreal forest species, it is isolated in the Black Hills with the nearest continuous population in the Northern Rocky Mountains or Northern Minnesota.

Wild Turkey. Photo courtesy B. J. Rose.

5. Turkey *Meleagris gallopavo* Linnaeus

An introduced permanent resident, now fairly common

110

throughout the Hills. Prefers pine forest and deciduous (oak) woodlands near open meadows or cultivated fields. Similar to the domestic turkey, but not so heavy and with a rusty tip to the tail. Roost in trees at night, will fly, but prefer to run, being excellent runners. Introduced to the Black Hills in the late forties and early fifties; now so well established that annual hunting seasons are allowed.

6. Northern Flicker (Red-shafted) *Colaptes auratus* (Linnaeus)

The most common woodpecker in the Hills, occurring at all elevations throughout the area. Identified by the reddish to orange wing and tail linings. Hybridizes freely with the yellow-shafted flicker to the extent that rarely does one find a true red or yellow form, most individuals being hybrids exhibiting varying shades of color. Prefers pine forests, streamside deciduous woodlands, or burns, also found in residential areas. Permanent resident, much more frequently encountered during the summer, but does occur occasionally in the winter.

7. Lewis' Woodpecker *Melanerpes lewis* (Gray)

A western form, identified by a red face and light collar and reddish underparts contrasting with the predominantly dark, greenish plumage of the back and wings; rump is black, larger than the red-headed woodpecker. Flight is slow with even flapping of the wings. One of the most interesting and colorful birds of the area. Occurs uncommonly as a summer resident and rarely as a winter resident. Prefers edges of pine forests or burns with dead upright trunks or stumps of trees for nests. Normally can be found in the McVey Burn-Slate Creek, Redfern area, migrates to lower elevations in the winter.

8. Western Wood Pewee *Contopus sordidulus* Sclater

A sparrow-sized flycatcher, dusky gray-brown above and lighter gray breast and sides, two narrow white wing-bars; a common summer resident at all elevations in the Black Hills, but particularly above 5000 ft. Frequently found in mature pine forests with large trees, typically do not occur in spruce forests; nest in tall trees, high

111

above the ground; a western form, probably does not extend east beyond the Black Hills.

9. Gray Jay   *Perisoreus canadensis* (Linnaeus)

A fairly common permanent resident at higher elevations throughout the Hills. Similar in size and general shape to the Blue Jay, but easily recognized by the black and white head and nape, generally gray body, lacking a crest. Habitually quiet, they may go unnoticed, but frequently appear around picnic or campgrounds where they seek table scraps, often coming close to tables or individuals. Sometimes called camp robbers or Canada Jay. Prefer dense coniferous forests, but also occur in mixed woodlands.

Black-billed Magpie. Photo courtesy Les Baylor.

10. Black-billed Magpie   *Pica pica* (Linnaeus)

A large black and white bird with a long sweeping tail, longer than the body. In flight the tail streams out behind and large white patches flash in the wing. A common permanent resident, more frequently encountered at lower elevations. Prefer open pine forests, deciduous woodlands or prairie groves. Most usually seen in flight in open country.

112

11. Pinyon Jay   *Gymnorhinus cyanocephalus* Wied

A fairly common permanent resident, at lower elevations throughout the Hills, typically between 3500 and 4500 ft. Prefer relatively open pine forests where the trees are smaller. Identified by a uniformly steel-blue color, short tail and long beak. Could be confused with the mountain bluebird, except for larger size and larger beak.

12. American Dipper (Water Oozle)   *Cinclus mexicanus* Swainson

One of the most interesting birds in the area, uniquely adapted to a watery habitat; strong legs and special oil glands allow them to walk under water as they feed, identified by slate-gray color, stubby tail and particularly a behavioral pattern of bobbing entire body up and down as they move along rocks in and near streams. A permanent resident of fast-flowing streams in the Hills, particularly in the central and northern region, probably most numerous in the Spearfish Canyon area; winter at lower

Dipper (Water Oozle). Photo courtesy B. J. Rose.

113

elevations. Not common, but inhabit certain areas repeatedly such as Roughlock Falls in Little Spearfish Canyon.

13. Rock Wren   *Salpinctes obsoletus* (Say)

A gray-backed wren with a buff rump, and light buff tips on tail with a subterminal black band; light streaks on breast. A fairly common summer resident at all elevations, prefers rocky outcrops, rough cliff walls and sharply-eroded slopes in dry areas. Usually can be found in the Red Valley and Hogback regions. Typically nests in crevices among rocks. A western form, reaches its eastern limit in the Black Hills.

Mountain Bluebird. Photo courtesy B. J. Rose.

14. Mountain Bluebird   *Sialia currucoides* (Bechstein)

One of the most common summer residents in the Hills,

114

occurring at all elevations, more commonly at higher elevations; doesn't seem to have a preference for habitat, occurring in most open areas such as meadows, wide canyons, burns, lumbered areas, clearings, cultivated fields with trees nearby for nesting. Readily recognized by the azure-blue color above, and lighter below, male with a blue breast, female gray; has a habit of hovering over the ground searching for insects, frequently perches on fences, telephone lines or power lines, blue color very apparent in flight. One of the colorful birds of the area.

15. Townsend's Solitaire   *Myadestes townsendi* (Audubon)

A small, gray-bodied bird that flycatches from a high perch in the open; song is a clear, musical warble; has a habit of performing a flight song, as it spirals above the tree tops hovering and singing loudly, then descending rapidly. The only member of this family to nest on the ground, preferring shelter of such things as heavy overhanging turf on edge of road cuts, deep cuts in broken rock or rocky shelves densely covered by vegetation. A fairly common permanent resident at all elevations throughout the Hills. Prefers pine and spruce forests, winters at lower elevations in woodlands.

16. Yellow-rumped Warbler   *Dendroica coronata auduboni*
(Audubon form)   (Townsend)

A dark blue-gray warbler with heavy black breast patch, throat, crown and side patches yellow with yellow rump and large white wing patches in male; female brown instead of gray and lacking wing patch. The western counterpart of the Myrtle, it resembles the Myrtle except for the yellow throat and white wing patch. A common summer resident at all elevations in the Black Hills, prefers coniferous forests, the only wood warbler breeding in pines.

17. Ovenbird   *Seiurus aurocapillus* (Linnaeus)

A ground-walking, ground-nesting warbler with plain olive upperparts, heavily-streaked breast and black stripes on crown, a rufous cap. Fairly common summer

115

resident at all elevations, prefers deciduous woodlands or mixed deciduous-coniferous forests. Frequently encountered in aspen-birch stands at lower edges of canyons or gullies where spruce and pine forests terminate. Commonly seen at lower elevations in wooded areas during migration.

18. Common Yellowthroat   *Geothlypis trichas* (Linnaeus)

An olive-backed warbler, male underparts yellow with distinctive black mark, female's chin, throat and breast more yellow than its belly which is dull white. Common summer resident at all elevations; prefers moist grassy or shrubby areas, occurring in streamside woody thickets, near open wet ground with sedges, rushes and tall herbs. More common in central and northern Hills.

19. Northern Oriole (Bullock's)   *Icterus galbula bullockii* (Swainson)

An intensely orange and black bird, with large white wing patches, smaller than a robin. Female similar to Baltimore Oriole female, olive-gray above, yellowish tail and underparts. The only oriole found in most sections of western United States, extending from the western edge of the great plains west. Fairly common summer resident at lower elevations in the Black Hills, prefers streamside thickets and large deciduous trees.

20. Western Tanager   *Piranga ludoviciana* (Wilson)

A distinctive, very colorful bird, yellow and black with a red face. Female dull green above and yellowish below; white wing bars in both sexes. A western form, common summer resident at all elevations in the Black Hills. Prefers pine forests, but can be found in deciduous woodlands along streams and in gullies and canyons. Usually nests in pine trees.

21. Black-headed Grosbeak   *Pheucticus melanocephalus* (Swainson)

The only grosbeak with orange underparts, a black head and white wing patches; the female is brown, has fine streaking on the sides and yellow wing linings. A western

116

Western Tanager. Photo courtesy Les Baylor.

form, it probably reaches its eastern limit in the Black Hills. Fairly common, it can be found at lower elevations and occasionally at higher elevations; prefers streamside deciduous woodlands. Fairly common in Spearfish Canyon in heavy shrub thickets.

22. Lazuli Bunting *Passerina amoena* (Say)

A small bright blue finch. Head and upper parts blue with an orange band across the breast and sides, white belly and white wing bars. Similar, except for smaller size and wing bars, to eastern bluebird. Female brownish, lighter on throat and belly. The western counterpart of the eastern Indigo Bunting; the two species overlap their ranges in the Black Hills and occupy almost identical habitats with a resultant frequent interbreeding; a com-

117

mon summer resident at lower elevations; prefers low deciduous thickets along streamside or in gullies or draws. Nests are usually in shrubs or small trees, three to six feet above ground.

23. Red Crossbill   *Loxia curvirostra* Linnaeus

The crossbills, as the name indicates, have a peculiar crossed bill which they use in extracting seeds from spruce and pine cones; the Red Crossbill is basically a red bird with black wings, distinguished from the white-winged crossbill by its lack of wing bars. The immature bird is more rust colored; the female is more yellowish with a yellow rump. Unpredictable as to occurrence, it varies from rare to very common seasonally in the Black Hills, probably dependent on the current crop of seeds in the conifers; although it can occur at any time of year it is more likely encountered during the winter. Prefers coniferous forests at all elevations. A northern form, it extends as far south as the Black Hills and as far as Arizona at higher elevations in the Rocky Mountains.

24. Dark-eyed (White-winged) Junco   *Junco aikeni* Ridgway

The only endemic subspecies occurring in the Black Hills, the White-winged Junco occurs very commonly at all elevations. Identified by sparrow-like, slate-gray body with two white wing bars and definite white edges on tail. Exhibits a definite spring and fall migration pattern, both altitudinally and latitudinally. Breeds in coniferous forests or in deciduous woodlands in canyons and gullies; winters in streamside deciduous woodlands or pine forests at lower elevations.

25. Chipping Sparrow   *Spizella passerina* (Bechstein)

A small, clear gray-breasted sparrow with a bright rufous cap, a black line through the eye and a white line over it. An abundant summer resident, one of the most numerous breeding birds at all elevations in the Black Hills. Breeds in open coniferous forests; in migration occupies

118

open woodlands or shrub thickets, or fields and roadsides along with other sparrows.

Several references are useful for the serious "birder" or the person who desires a field guide to the birds of the area. The best source for providing information on the occurrence, local status, distribution, habitats, nesting and migration of birds in the Black Hills is Pettingill and Whitney, *Birds of the Black Hills.** It is more useful to the competent "birder" than the beginner since it does not include photographs or drawings for identification purposes. Unfortunately it is now out of print; therefore it is not readily available. The ever-popular Peterson series is excellent; however, since the majority of the birds are western, the *Field Guide to Western Birds*** is more appropriate than the *Field Guide to the Birds.* The more recently published *Birds of North America,**** a well-illustrated field guide, is also excellent and useful in the entire area. The Forest Service has published a *Checklist of Birds in the Black Hills National Forest,* (U.S.D.A., Forest Service, 1972). Copies may be secured from any official Forest Service station in the Hills. These are useful for recording personal daily counts, but are, of course, merely checklists. They do include the resident status of each species. A similar checklist is available on the *Birds of the Buffalo Gap National Grasslands;* this checklist is appropriate for the entire Great Plains area surrounding the Hills.

Pettingill and Whitney, in their *Birds of the Black Hills,* originally proposed a system for seasonally classifying the birds of the area based on resident or transient status. This is a most useful tool and method for the field student. A modification of their original system has been used in the following checklist, employing only four of their categories (permanent residents,

---

*Pettingill, Olin Sewall, Jr. and Nathaniel R. Whitney, Jr. 1965. *Birds of the Black Hills.* Special Publication No. 1 Cornell Laboratory of Ornithology, Cornell University, Ithaca, N.Y.

**Peterson, Roger Tory. 1961. *Field Guide to Western Birds.* Houghton-Mifflin Co., Boston, Mass. 366 pp.

***Robbins, Chandler, S., Bertel Brunn & Herbert S. Zim. 1966. *Birds of North America.* Golden Press, New York; Western Publishing Co., Inc., Ramil, Wis. 340 pp.

summer residents, winter residents, and transients). The rare category has been eliminated . . . it is used, where appropriate, for individual species, under each of the four main groups. Also, this checklist differs in many respects from other checklists, being based on more recent records and information. It was prepared with the generous and competent aid of Les Baylor, Rapid City, S.D., a well-known local ornithologist and authority on the birds of the Black Hills area. The list and descriptive information is based largely on Baylor's field notes and observations generally covering the past decade.

The categories used should be interpreted in this way:

Permanent residents = species that are present the year round and breeding regularly.

Summer residents = species present during the summer, absent or rare in winter, and breeding regularly.

Transients = species that pass through the Hills during migration; some species may be an occasional summer or winter resident.

Winter resident = species that appear in the Hills at any time during the winter, usually northern species.

The South Dakota Ornithologists' Union (S.D.O.U.) published a revised edition of The Birds of South Dakota in 1991. Originally published in 1978, this revised edition changes the sequence of some birds and updates the nomenclature. The professional ornithologist, or avid "birder," may wish to consult this new list for detailed information on the birds of the area.

The following list of birds of the Black Hills follows the sequence and terminology of the new edition.

In addition, copies of the S.D.O.U. Field Checklist of Birds of South Dakota are also available (Rt. 4, Box 252, Brookings, S.D. 57006).

BIRDS OF THE BLACK HILLS

PERMANENT RESIDENTS

Common Name	Scientific Name

Mallard — *Anas platyrhynchos* L.

Fairly common near lakes, ponds and larger streams.

Sharp-shinned Hawk — *Accipiter striatus* Vieillot

Fairly common in deciduous or coniferous woodlands.

Cooper's Hawk — *Accipiter cooperii* Bonaparte

Uncommon to rare in deciduous or coniferous woodlands.

Northern Goshawk — *Accipiter gentilis* L.

Uncommon at higher elevations in pine forests.

Golden Eagle — *Aquila chrysaëtos* L.

Uncommon to rare near rocky cliffs or open prairies; more frequently found in Wind Cave National Park and Custer State Park.

Prairie Falcon — *Falco mexicanus* Schlegel

Uncommon in canyons with sheer cliffs.

Ring-necked Pheasant — *Phasianus colchicus* L.

Uncommon in grasslands or thickets near streams.

Ruffed Grouse — *Bonasa umbellus* L.

Uncommon, found at all elevations in aspen groves or mixed deciduous-coniferous woodlands.

Sharp-tailed Grouse — *Tympanuchus phasianellus* L.

Fairly common in mountain prairies and grassland-aspen habitats; usually can be found in McVey Burn area.

Ruffed Grouse. Photo courtesy Les Baylor.

Turkey   *Meleagris gallopavo* L.

Introduced, fairly common in open pine forest with heavy ground cover of grasses.

Great Horned Owl   *Bubo virginianus* Gmelin

Common at all elevations in woodlands.

Belted Kingfisher   *Ceryle alcyon* L.

Common near lakes, ponds, and streams; frequently seen in Cleghorn Springs Fish Hatchery area, west of Rapid City.

Downy Woodpecker   *Picoides pubescens* L.

Fairly common at all elevations, less numerous than the Hairy Woodpecker; prefers deciduous woodlands.

Hairy Woodpecker   *Picoides villosus* L.

Common at all elevations in deciduous or coniferous woodlands.

Three-toed Woodpecker　　　　　　　*Picoides tridactylus* L.

Rare at higher elevations in spruce forest of northern and west-central areas.

Black-backed Woodpecker　　　　　*Picoides arcticus* Swainson

Present in small numbers at higher elevations in coniferous forests.

Gray Jay　　　　　　　　　　　　*Perisoreus canadensis* L.

Fairly common at elevations above 4,000 ft. in dense coniferous forest.

Blue Jay　　　　　　　　　　　　*Cyanocitta cristata* L.

Common in deciduous woodlands at lower elevations, possibly at elevations up to 5,000 ft.; prefers bur oak habitat.

Pinyon Jay　　　　　　　*Gymnorhinus cyanocephalus* Wied

Common at lower elevations from 3,500 to 4,500 ft. in relatively open pine forests, especially in the foothills of west Rapid City.

Black-billed Magpie　　　　　　　　　　*Pica pica* L.

Common in open grasslands and sometimes in open forest areas; more numerous at lower elevations.

American Crow　　　　　*Corvus brachyrhynchos* Brehm

Common spring and fall transient, fairly common in summer, not so common in winter; in forest and grassland habitats.

Black-capped Chickadee　　　　　　*Parus atricapillus* L.

Abundant at all elevations in deciduous or coniferous habitats.

Red-breasted Nuthatch　　　　　　*Sitta canadensis* L.

Common in coniferous forest, but also in mixed coniferous-deciduous forests.

White-breasted Nuthatch　　　　　*Sitta carolinensis* Latham

Fairly common in pine forests and mixed pine-deciduous woodlands.

Pigmy Nuthatch　　　　　　　　*Sitta pygmaea* Vigors

Uncommon resident, recently reported more regularly, in pine forests.

Brown Creeper　　　　　　　　　*Certhia americana* Bonaparte

Uncommon, more conspicuous in winter, in coniferous or mixed forests.

American Dipper　　　　　　　　　*Cinclus mexicanus* Swainson

Fairly common in certain locations, particularly along fast-flowing, tumbling streams in the northern Hills, such as Spearfish Creek and Roughlock Falls.

Golden-crowned Kinglet　　　　　　　　　*Regulus satrapa* L.

Uncommon, found at higher elevations in spruce forest.

Townsend's Solitaire　　　　　　　　　*Myadestes townsendi* Audubon

Common at all elevations; coniferous forest in summer, mixed forest in winter; comes to residential areas in winter.

Cedar Waxwing　　　　　　　　　*Bombycilla cedrorum* Vieillot

Rare to uncommon at lower elevations, more numerous in spring and fall than other times; prefers deciduous woodland, especially fruit or berry trees.

Starling　　　　　　　　　*Sturnus vulgaris* L.

Fairly common at lower elevations, generally associated with buildings.

Song Sparrow　　　　　　　　　*Melospiza melodia* Wilson

Fairly common among low shrubs and trees near streams and cat-tail marshes.

Dark-eyed Junco　　　　　　　　　*Junco hyemalis aikeni* Ridgway
(White-winged Junco)

Very common at all elevations; prefers relatively open pine forest.

Cassins' Finch　　　　　　　　　*Carpodacus cassinii* Baird

Fairly common in residential areas and pine forests, with few remaining as summer residents in pine forests.

House Finch　　　　　　　　　*Carpodacus mexicanus* Muller

Uncommon, sporadic; records from all seasons.

124

Red Crossbill *Loxia curvirostra* L.

Numbers fluctuate significantly with cone or seed production years; associated with pine forests.

Pine Siskin *Carduelis pinus* Wilson

Abundant, conspicuous at all times of year, migrate to lower elevations in the winter; prefer coniferous forest but also found in deciduous woodland.

American Goldfinch *Carduelis tristis* L.

Common summer resident at lower elevations, uncommon winter resident; primarily associated with deciduous woodlands, but often feeds in weedy-grassy areas.

Evening Grosbeak *Coccothraustes vespertinus* Cooper

Common winter resident and spring and fall transient; some individuals remaining as summer residents in deciduous and coniferous forest.

House Sparrow *Passer domesticus* L.

Abundant everywhere.

SUMMER RESIDENTS

Turkey Vulture *Cathartes aura* L.

Fairly common to common, more likely seen at lower elevations, soaring high over forest canopy or mountain prairies.

Red-tailed Hawk *Buteo jamaicensis* Gmelin

Common, the most conspicuous and probably the most numerous hawk in the Black Hills during the summer, a few may remain in winter; frequents open areas of forest edges and meadows.

American Kestrel (Sparrow Hawk) *Falco sparverius* L.

Common at all elevations; readily seen in open areas of meadows, valleys and canyons.

Killdeer *Charadrius vociferus* L.

Common in summer, rare in winter; frequents open cultivated areas and sandy or muddy shores of ponds and lakes.

Spotted Sandpiper *Actitis macularia* L.

Common along streams, ponds and rocky lake shores.

Mourning Dove *Zenaidura macroura* L.

Common to locally abundant in all habitats.

Black-billed Cuckoo *Coccyzus erythropthalmus* Wilson

Uncommon, at lower elevations in relatively dense deciduous woodlands.

Common Nighthawk *Chordeiles minor* Forster

Common, most numerous at lower elevations over forests and cities.

Common Poor-will *Phalaenoptilus nuttallii* Audubon

Fairly common in summer, apparently restricted to pine forests at lower elevations, especially near Rapid City.

White-throated Swift *Aëronautes saxatalis* Woodhouse

Common, readily seen in Strato Bowl, Dark Canyon and Spearfish Canyon.

Lewis' Woodpecker *Melanerpes lewis* Gray

Conspicuous summer resident in modest numbers in major burn areas such as the McVey and Deadwood burns; prefers tall dead trees. Rare winter resident in cottonwood stands at lower elevations.

Red-headed Woodpecker *Melanerpes erythrocephalus* L.

Uncommon, generally restricted to deciduous woodlands at lower elevations.

Red-naped Sapsucker *Sphyrapicus nuchalis* Baird

Uncommon summer resident.

Northern Flicker (Red-shafted Flicker) *Colaptes auratus* L.

Common at all elevations in pine or deciduous forests, most numerous woodpecker in Black Hills, occasional winter resident.

Western Wood Pewee *Contopus sordidulus* Sclater

Common to abundant, at all elevations, especially between 5,000 and 6,000 ft.; prefers pine forest or mixed forest habitat and streamside.

Dusky Flycatcher *Empidonax oberholseri* Phillips

Fairly common in Spearfish Canyon, and aspen groves on McVey Burn.

Cordilleran Flycatcher *Empidonax occidentalis* Nelson

Common throughout the Black Hills, prefers streamsides or moist areas in coniferous or mixed forests.

Say's Phoebe *Sayornis saya* Bonaparte

Uncommon near open areas, farmsteads, abandoned buildings and bridges at lower elevations.

Western Kingbird *Tyrannus verticalis* Say

Fairly common near open areas, farmsteads, and along roadsides at lower elevations.

Eastern Kingbird *Tyrannus tyrannus* L.

Common near open areas, fields and along streams and roads at lower elevations; the most conspicuous flycatcher around Rapid City.

Horned Lark *Eremophila alpestris* L.

Fairly common at all elevations, in mountain grasslands such as Reynolds Prairie and Wind Cave National Park.

Tree Swallow *Iridoprocne bicolor* Vieillot

Uncommon; prefers deciduous habitats and open areas near residences.

Violet-green Swallow *Tachycineta thalassina* Swainson

Common at all elevations, the most numerous swallow in the Black Hills; prefers steep canyons; often feeds over meadows, lakes, ponds and streams.

Northern Rough-winged Swallow *Stelgidopteryx serripennis* Audubon

Common near Rapid City, uncommon elsewhere; feeds near streams, ponds, lakes.

Cliff Swallow *Hirundo pyrrhonota* Vieillot

Uncommon near meadows, streams and lakes, usually in canyons, nests under bridges and eaves of buildings.

Barn Swallow   *Hirundo rustica* L.

Uncommon, near fields and meadows, lakes and streams, nests under bridges and eaves of buildings.

Rock Wren   *Salpinctes obsoletus* Say

Uncommon to common, at all elevations; frequents rocky outcrops, cliffs and rocky slopes of open pine forests.

Canyon Wren   *Catherpes mexicanus* Swainson

Uncommon, in deep canyons and steep rocky hillsides in pine forests; rare winter resident, more conspicuous in spring and fall.

House Wren   *Troglodytes aedon* Vieillot

Common at lower elevations, prefers deciduous thickets and woods, especially near streams and residential areas.

Eastern Bluebird   *Sialia sialis* L.

Uncommon to rare along pine forest edges and streamside woods at lower elevations.

Mountain Bluebird   *Sialia currucoides* Bechstein

Very common at all elevations, prefers pine forest edges and mountain meadows and prairies.

Veery   *Catharus fuscescens* Stephens

Fairly common in dense deciduous habitat in Spearfish Canyon, but uncommon to rare elsewhere.

Swainson's Thrush   *Catharus ustulatus* Nuttall

Fairly common in spruce and mixed coniferous-deciduous habitats along major streams at higher elevations.

American Robin   *Turdus migratorius* L.

Abundant, found in virtually all types of habitats at all elevations, rare winter resident or visitant.

Gray Catbird   *Dumetella carolinensis* L.

Fairly common in dense deciduous habitats near streams at lower elevations.

Brown Thrasher *Toxostoma rufum* L.

Fairly common in deciduous habitats near streams and in residential areas at elevations below 4,000 feet.

Loggerhead Shrike *Lanius ludovicianus* L.

Rare to uncommon in open areas near deciduous habitats at lower elevations.

Solitary Vireo *Vireo solitarius* Wilson

Common in pine forest or mixed pine-aspen habitats at all elevations.

Warbling Vireo *Vireo gilvus* Vieillot

Common at all elevations, generally confined to relatively dense deciduous habitats.

Red-eyed Vireo *Vireo olivaceus* L.

Common, frequents the upper canopy of deciduous woodlands along streams and in residential areas at lower elevations.

Yellow Warbler *Dendroica petechia* L.

Very common in deciduous habitats, especially cottonwoods and elms in the foothills, uncommon at higher elevations.

Yellow-rumped Warbler *Dendroica coronata auduboni*
(Audubon form) Townsend

Common in spruce and pine forests at all elevations.

American Redstart *Setophaga ruticilla* L.

Fairly common in deciduous thickets along streams at lower to moderately high elevations.

Ovenbird *Seiurus aurocapillus* L.

Fairly common at all elevations, prefers dense deciduous or mixéd deciduous-coniferous woodlands especially in gulches and canyons.

MacGillivray's Warbler *Oporornis tolmiei* Townsend

Uncommon to rare in deciduous habitats of streams, canyons and gulches.

Common Yellowthroat (Yellowthroat) *Geothlypis trichas* L.

Common in deciduous thickets along streams and marshes at all elevations.

Yellow-breasted Chat *Icteria virens* L.

Fairly common in dense deciduous thickets along streams and in gulches and draws at lower elevations.

Western Tanager *Piranga ludoviciana* Wilson

Common at all elevations, prefers pine forest but also occurs in mixed coniferous-deciduous habitats.

Black-headed Grosbeak *Pheucticus melanocephalus* Swainson

Fairly common, frequenting deciduous habitats along streams and in residential areas, mainly at lower elevations.

Red-winged Blackbird *Agelaius phoeniceus* L.

Common near marshes, ponds, lakes, streams and meadows at all elevations.

Western Meadowlark *Sturnella neglecta* Audubon

Abundant, in open grasslands at lower elevations and on mountain prairies, rare in winter.

Brewer's Blackbird *Euphagus cyanocephalus* Wagler

Fairly common in open fields and meadows at lower elevations and on mountain prairies.

Common Grackle *Quiscalus quiscula* L.

Common near woodlands and in residential areas at lower elevations, uncommon to rare at higher elevations.

Orchard Oriole *Icterus spuriús* L.

Uncommon in deciduous habitat and in residential areas and parks of cities, no nesting records.

Northern Oriole *Icterus galbula bullockii* Swainson
(Bullock's Oriole)

Fairly common in deciduous habitats, especially cottonwoods along streams at lower elevations.

130

Lazuli Bunting *Passerina amoena* Say

Fairly common in deciduous habitats at lower elevations especially in thickets near streams.

Indigo Bunting *Passerina cyanea* L.

Rare to uncommon in deciduous habitats at lower elevations, especially along streams.

Rufous-sided Towhee *Pipilo erythrophthalmus* L.

Common at all elevations, prefers dense deciduous thickets in gulches and draws.

Chipping Sparrow *Spizella passerina* Bechstein

Abundant at all elevations, primarily associated with open coniferous habitats.

Vesper Sparrow *Pooecetes gramineus* Gmelin

Fairly common in meadows and grasslands, probably nests regularly in the McVey Burn area and mountain prairies.

Lark Sparrow *Chondestes grammacus* Say

Common at lower elevations, prefers open, dry grasslands and arid slopes near forest edges.

Lark Bunting *Calamospiza melanocorys* Stejneger

Uncommon is open grasslands at lower elevations, rare in open areas at higher elevations; can be found in the Red Valley.

TRANSIENTS

Pied-billed Grebe *Podilymbus podiceps* L.

Uncommon in spring and fall at lakes and ponds.

Eared Grebe *Podiceps nigricollis* Brehm

Uncommon in spring and fall at larger lakes, occasional winter visitant.

Canada Goose *Branta canadensis* L.

Fairly common in spring and fall at lakes and ponds, occasional winter resident.

Green-winged Teal   *Anas crecca* L.

Uncommon in spring and fall at lakes, ponds and marshes.

Northern Pintail   *Anas acuta* L.

Uncommon in spring and fall at lakes, ponds and marshes, rare winter visitant.

Blue-winged Teal   *Anas discors* L.

Uncommon in spring and fall at lakes, ponds and marshes; occasional summer resident.

Northern Shoveler (Shoveler)   *Anas clypeata* L.

Common spring and fall at lakes, ponds and marshes.

American Wigeon (Widgeon)   *Anas americana* Gmelin

Fairly common spring and fall at lakes, ponds and marshes; summer resident, rare winter visitant.

Canvasback   *Aythya valisineria* Wilson

Uncommon spring and fall, primarily on deep lakes; occasional winter resident.

Redhead   *Aythya americana* Eyton

Uncommon spring and fall, primarily on deep lakes; occasionally in winter.

Lesser Scaup   *Aythya affinis* Eyton

Common spring and fall, primarily on deep lakes, uncommon winter resident.

Ruddy Duck   *Oxyura jamaicensis* Gmelin

Uncommon fall transient at lakes and ponds.

Osprey   *Pandion haliaetus* L.

Uncommon, near lakes and streams.

Northern Harrier   *Circus cyaneus* L.

Uncommon spring and fall in open grasslands at lower elevations, rare summer resident in the more open lower valleys.

American Coot   *Fulica americana* L.

Spring and fall on lakes, ponds, and marshes; rare summer and winter visitant.

Sandhill Crane   *Grus canadensis* L.

Most often seen in migratory flight, especially in autumn along the foothills, but also over the interior of the Hills; may pause to feed in moist grasslands.

Solitary Sandpiper   *Tringa solitaria* Wilson

Uncommon spring and fall near streams, marshes and ponds.

Winter Wren   *Troglodytes troglodytes* L.

Uncommon spring and fall in dense thickets in canyons and along streams; occasional winter resident.

Orange-crowned Warbler   *Vermivora celata* Say

Uncommon spring and rare fall in deciduous habitats along streams and in residential areas.

Yellow-rumped Warbler (Myrtle form)   *Dendroica coronata* L.

Uncommon spring and rare fall in deciduous habitats near streams and in residential areas.

Rose-breasted Grosbeak   *Pheucticus ludovicianus* L.

Fairly rare spring at lower elevations.

Clay-colored Sparrow   *Spizella pallida* Swainson

Common spring and fall, rare summer resident in pastures, fields and pine-forest edges.

Savannah Sparrow   *Passerculus sandwichensis* Gmelin

Uncommon to rare spring and fall in grassland prairies and meadows.

Lincoln's Sparrow   *Melospiza lincolnii* Audubon

Uncommon spring and fall in streamside thickets and dense deciduous woodlands.

White-crowned Sparrow   *Zonotrichia leucophrys* Forster

Common spring and fall in streamside thickets and dense deciduous woodlands.

Brown-headed Cowbird *Molothrus ater* Boddaert

Uncommon spring and fall, fairly common summer resident at lower elevations in pastures and fields, streamside thickets.

WINTER RESIDENTS

Gadwall *Anas strepera* L.

Common in winter and spring, and fall transient, on open water of lakes, ponds and streams.

Common Goldeneye *Bucephala clangula* L.

Common in winter on open water of lakes, ponds and streams.

Hooded Merganser *Lophodytes cucullatus* L.

Winter resident in small numbers on open water of lakes.

Common Merganser *Mergus merganser* L.

Common in winter on open water of lakes, casual summer visitant or resident.

Bald Eagle *Haliaeetus leucocephalus* L.

Uncommon near open water of streams and lakes, mountain valleys and prairies.

Rough-legged Hawk *Buteo lagopus* Pontoppidan

Uncommon in winter in grasslands and prairies.

Bohemian Waxwing *Bombycilla garrulus* L.

Sporadic winter visitant, prefers trees retaining fruit or berries.

American Tree Sparrow *Spizella arborea* Wilson

Common winter resident and transient in deciduous habitats and weed fields at lower elevations, utilizes residential feeding stations.

Dark-eyed Junco (Slate-colored Junco) *Junco hyemalis* L.

Fairly common, frequently deciduous and coniferous habitats and utilizes residential feeding stations.

Dark-eyed Junco (Oregon Junco) *Junco oreganus* Townsend

Common, frequents deciduous and coniferous habitats and utilizes residential feeding stations.

Rosy Finch *Leucosticte arctoa* Pallas

Sporadic winter visitant in open areas of coniferous habitats; when present may occur in flocks of twenty or more.

Purple Finch *Carpodacus purpureus* Gmelin

Irregular in small numbers in residential areas.

Common Redpoll *Carduelis flammea* L.

Uncommon in deciduous thickets, week fields and pine forests.

MAMMALS OF THE BLACK HILLS

Among the major animal groups, undoubtedly the mammals enjoy the greatest popularity and are of more general interest to most people, particularly children, than the other types of animals. This is to be expected since many mammals are larger and thus more visible than such groups as amphibians, reptiles and birds. In addition people are more familiar with mammals through contacts such as domestication, zoos, and other educational experiences.

In the Black Hills area, game preserves in Wind Cave National Park, Custer State Park and The Badlands National Monument support fairly large populations of mammals, particularly the more striking big game animals. In these situations they can be observed and studied quite easily under relatively natural conditions. The parks are sufficiently large to produce near natural open conditions and support large herds. Herds or

Bull Elk. Photo courtesy Kent Fish, 1976.

individual bison, wapiti (elk), pronghorn (antelope), mountain sheep and mountain goats, are quite commonly encountered in

136

one or both of the parks or other preserves. The white-tail deer is the most common large mammal in the Hills proper, ranging throughout the Hills at all elevations as well as the surrounding Plains. The mule deer, preferring an open rolling type habitat, is not so common in the Hills proper, occurring at higher elevations in more rugged areas in the western and southwestern parts, as well as in the breaks and rocky ridges of the surrounding high Plains. Elk occur, less commonly than deer, but are restricted to higher, more remote elevations of the limestone plateau, and in rougher terrain near the parks. The pronghorn (antelope) rarely occurs in the Hills proper, but is relatively common throughout the surrounding high Plains area, particularly to the west and north of the Hills (northwestern South Dakota, Wyoming and Montana). The remaining big game types may occasionally escape and be seen outside preserves, but this would represent a rare occurrence.

White-tail Doe and Fawn. Photo courtesy Kent Fish, 1976.

137

Among the species considered as native to the Hills are two that most probably no longer occur here. The grizzly bear has not been reported since the late 1800's, and the gray wolf, one of the most common animals in the Hills during the 1800's, was last reported in 1928. Since there have been no reports of either species during a period of nearly 50 years, it can be assumed they no longer occur here. In addition there are four species that are extremely rare although reported occasionally, almost always on the basis of sight records or tracks. Included in this category are the mountain lion, black bear, lynx and the black-footed ferret (currently listed as an endangered species).

The most recent mountain lion specimen taken in the Hills was in 1958 on Elk Mountain in Custer County. There have been sight records and tracks reported occasionally since then. The author has personally seen mountain lions on two fairly recent occasions. In June, 1969 one was observed, within 50 yards, in the Limestone area, west of Bear Mountain near the Custer-Pennington County line. Another was observed in late July, 1975 a few miles north of the first sighting. Both observations were clear sightings, witnessed by several persons travelling in the same car.

At one time the black bear was fairly common in the Black Hills. Apparently it has almost disappeared. However, it has been reported from time to time. The most recent sightings have come from different localities including: Big Spearfish Canyon; Cold Creek in Lawrence Co.; Redfern, Pennington Co.; Beaver Creek Valley in Pennington Co.; near Rochford, Pennington Co.; and between Black Fox Campground and Crook's Tower in western Lawrence Co. On the basis of such reports, plus occasional newspaper accounts of sightings, and other sources, it is safe to assume that the black bear still exists, although rare, in the Black Hills.

The lynx is another rare species that occurs in the Black Hills area. In fact it was probably never very common, but it has been taken on occasion in recent years. One record from Meade County in 1944 and two from Pennington County in 1945 plus two additional records from the northern and western Black

138

Hills in the last 10 years verify its presence. It has to be considered as an occasional migrant or very rare resident.

The black-footed ferret remains as one of the rarest of the mammals on the continent. It is present in southwestern South Dakota, and probably still exists in the foothills in the southeastern Black Hills, notably in Wind Cave National Park and possibly Custer State Park. Since it preys primarily on the prairie dog, its distribution is generally restricted to localities where prairie dog towns exist. Owing to the fact that it is primarily nocturnal and therefore extremely difficult to observe, no one really knows the current status of the ferret. Experts working on the species report that they may work several years and actually see very few individuals, even though they are doing research in prairie dog towns. It is generally assumed that the ferret is barely holding its own in South Dakota.

There are 62 species of mammals that presently occur in the Black Hills, representing 44 genera, 19 families and 6 orders. Among the 62 are included: 59 indigenous (native) species, 4 species of which were previously extirpated and reintroduced (the bison, pronghorn, mountain sheep and wapiti [elk]), and 1 species, the fox squirrel, was probably introduced but most likely also reached the Hills along natural routes of dispersal; and 3 species introduced, directly or indirectly, by man are not, nor ever were, native (mountain goat, Norway rat and the house mouse). In addition there are 19 species that must be listed as questionable . . . they have either been reported from the Hills in the literature and are not present, or they have been recently collected from the immediate high plains area surrounding the Hills.

It is difficult to categorize or generalize in regard to distributions or "life-zones" inhabited by the mammalian fauna in the Hills. The range of some species is restricted to certain specific areas such as: the mountain goat in the Harney Range-Rushmore area, the bison in Custer State Park and Wind Cave National Park, and the black-footed ferret in prairie dog towns. However, generally speaking and within the restrictions of habitat availability, most of the mammals that occur are distributed over a wider range, frequently throughout the Hills proper. This is particularly due to the topographic and climatic nature of the Hills plus the vegetational mixture present here, being a mountainous upthrust surrounded by high Plains grasslands. Moreover, as with the vegetation, the native mammal species that occur here are a mixture of several faunal divisions or units.

In their comprehensive biogeographic analysis of the recent mammalian fauna of the northern Great Plains, Hoffman and Jones* have classified the Black Hills mammals according to faunal units.

Twenty-six species (37.1%) of the Black Hills mammals are classified as *Widespread Species* meaning that they have no apparent faunal affinities with the Hills, but are present because they are extremely mobile and have a wide range of tolerance for environmental factors. Included in this category are such types as some of the bats, large ungulates and carnivores. Ten species (14.3%) are classified as *Steppe Species* and have evolved in response to the semi-arid to arid environment of the Great Plains area and are closely allied with this biota. The white-tailed jackrabbit, black-footed ferret, and thirteen-lined ground squirrel are examples of this group.

Ten additional species (14.3%) are classed as *Boreomontane Species*, distributed both in the northern boreal forest and in the coniferous forest of western montane areas. Mammals belonging to this faunal unit range much farther north than do members of the Cordilleran unit; they also do not extend as far south. Some of the members of this faunal unit represent "glacial relicts" that were probably isolated with the retreat of the ice sheets. The marten, Canada lynx, and ermine belong to this unit.

The *Cordilleran Species*, also represented by ten species (14.3%), includes elements probably displaced into the region by Cordilleran (Rocky Mountain) ice sheets. The mountain

---

*Hoffman, R. S. and J. K. Jones, Jr. 1970. *Influence of the Late Glacial and Past Glacial Events on the Distribution of Recent Mammals in the Northern Great Plains.* pp. 355-394, *in* Pleistocene and Recent Environments of the Central and Great Plains (W. Dort, Jr. and J. K. Jones, ed.) Kansas University Press, Lawrenee,Kansas. 433 pp.

sheep, yellow-bellied marmot and Nuttall's cottontail are representative of this unit. Most of the Rocky Mountain forms attain their easternmost limits in the Black Hills.

In addition to these four faunal units, three smaller groups are represented in the Black Hills: the *Sonoran Species* consisting of 7 species (10%), represented by such forms as Ord's kangaroo rat, the western harvest mouse and the desert cottontail, a southwestern United States element, obviously migrating into the Hills in times of post- or inter-glacial warmth and dryness; the *Deciduous Forest Species,* numbering 6 species (8.6%) including the fox squirrel and eastern cottontail, and having affinities with eastern hardwood forests, mesic grasslands, or prairie riparian species . . . most of these forms reach their western limit in the Black Hills; finally, only one species (1.4%), the least chipmunk, belonging to the *Great Basin Species,* is also present here.

It should be noted that their classification, based on biogeographic affinities with counterparts elsewhere on the continent includes all recorded and reported species that definitely exist in the Black Hills currently, once occurred here, or are forms of uncertain status at the present time; hence the total of 70 species.

From this analysis it can readily be seen that the Black Hills mammalian fauna is, indeed, a most interesting and complex mixture. Thus, so far as their distributions in the Hills are concerned, one can only generalize. Individual species inhabit those situations in the Hills to which they are most favorably adapted. Therefore, for the most part, the Limestone Plateau and Central areas support basically a Boreomontane and Cordilleran mammal fauna, with their associated species attaining their highest population densities in these regions. The Red Valley, Minnekahta Plains and the outer rim of the Hogback, as well as the foothills, support basically a Steppe faunal element with some mixing of the Sonoran unit. The Deciduous Species element is primarily associated with the deciduous vegetation of the canyons, and drainage systems of lower elevations. The Widespread Species occur everywhere in the Hills. Thus, with the mixture that is present, coupled with the overlap of habitat so character-

141

istic of the Hills, it is understandable that the study of mammal distributions in the Black Hills is complicated. One can, indeed, expect to find a given native species nearly anywhere in the Hills, particularly under conditions of seasonal extreme weather patterns.

A complete checklist of the mammals of the Black Hills can be found on p. 146. Although it is not possible to include descriptions and the current status of all the mammals that occur here, notes of general interest for twenty selected species are included below. These were selected on the basis of personal experience and/or those forms that typically attract the most interest, questions and comments from students or visitors to the Hills. Included are brief accounts of their present status, relative abundance, general distribution or where one could reasonably expect to locate them, and a brief statement on preferred habitat.

TWENTY SELECTED MAMMALIAN SPECIES IN THE BLACK HILLS

Common Name	Scientific Name

1. Least Chipmunk — *Eutamias minimus silvaticus* White

   Native to Black Hills, common and widespread in wooded lowlands and surrounding Plains, most numerous in forested uplands, less dense in southern foothills and Hogback.

2. Black-tailed Prairie Dog — *Cynomys ludovicianus ludovicianus* Ord

   Native, inhabiting dry upland prairies, abundant in Wind Cave National Park.

3. Red Squirrel — *Tamiasciurus hudsonicus dakotensis* J. A. Allen

   Native, common in the northern and central Hills, found at elevations above 3800 ft., most numerous above 5200 ft.

142

4. Northern Flying Squirrel   *Glaucomys sabrinus bangsi*
                                                    Rhoads

Native, most abundant in spruce forests of moist canyon systems in the north, ranging down to 4500 ft.

Beaver Dam in Black Fox Canyon. Photo by author, 1973.

5. Beaver   *Castor canadensis missouriensis* Bailey

Originally native to this area, much less abundant now with some introduced stocks. Found on every major creek or river in South Dakota, but most numerous in Black Hills. Habitat consists of streams and lakes with trees or shrubs on banks.

6. Porcupine   *Erethizon dorsatum bruneri* Swenk

Occur in Great Plains where trees are available locally. Wide altitudinal distribution, common in the Hills.

7. Coyote   *Canis latrans latrans* Say

Widely distributed in Black Hills and surrounding Plains, increasing in abundance in northern Hills, especially along South Dakota-Wyoming border. Found in prairies, open woodlands and brushy areas.

143

8. Black Bear *Ursus americanus americanus* Pallas

Inhabiting mountainous areas, the black bear at one time was very abundant and native to the Hills, but now is disappearing and considered rare.

9. Raccoon *Procyon lotor hirtus* Nelson and Goldman

Common in the Black Hills, found along streams, around lakes and marshes and is a recent addition to the Black Hills fauna, not being native to this area.

10. Badger *Taxidea taxus taxus* Schreber

Occurs throughout the Red Valley and Wind Cave National Park as a common inhabitant. Not normally found in the Hills proper, the badger prefers open grasslands.

11. Mountain Lion *Felis concolor hippolestes* Merriam

Occurs, although quite uncommonly, inhabiting remote and rugged areas of the Black Hills.

12. Bobcat *Lynx rufus pallescens* Merriam

Abundant in the Hills region, the bobcat is common in the foothills, forested canyons and along wooded streams. Distribution is widespread.

13. Wapiti (Elk) *Cervus canadensis canadensis* Erxleben

A native species to the Hills, elk were reintroduced after extermination by man. Consisting of a northern herd in the Limestone area, and southern herd located in Wind Cave National Park and Custer Park, elk occupy forests in daylight hours and enter valley meadows in the early evening.

14. Mule Deer *Odocoileus hemionus hemionus* Rafinesque

An abundant native in the early days, mule deer are now declining in population. Inhabit open plains, broken country and brush or woods, greatest concentrations in the southern portion of the Hills.

15. White-tail Deer *Odocoileus virginianus dacotensis* Goldman and Kellogg

Widely distributed throughout the Hills, once an abundant native, but populations are somewhat depressed now, occurring in woodland areas, along forest edges and in thickets along streams.

16. Pronghorn (Antelope) *Antilocapra americana americana* Ord

Found in open prairies and sagebrush, once native to the Hills but greatly reduced in numbers today. Present in Wind Cave National Park, Custer State Park and Plains surrounding the Hills.

17. Bison (Buffalo) *Bison bison bison* Linnaeus

Native, once extremely abundant, nearly exterminated by 1900, then reintroduced. Currently large herds located in Wind Cave National Park and Custer State Park, inhabit open Plains.

18. Mountain Goat *Oreamnos americanus missoulae* J. A. Allen

Not originally native, an introduced species now inhabiting Mount Rushmore-Needles-Harney Peak area. Found where moss- and lichen-covered granitic ridges are present, steep slopes and usually above timberline.

19. Mountain Sheep *Ovis canadensis auduboni* Merriam

A different subspecies introduced after the original native subspecies was exterminated. Occur on rough buttes and canyons in more rugged mountains, presently chiefly located in Custer State Park.

20. Yellow-bellied Marmot *Marmota flaviventris dacota* Merriam

Not occurring in the Plains proper, restricted to mountains, foothills and rocky canyons. A native species, found only in the Black Hills and Wyoming; inhabits rocky hillsides, crevices in bluffs or rockpiles in meadows.

145

For more detailed description and other information on the mammals of the area, Turner's *Mammals of the Black Hills of South Dakota and Wyoming** is highly recommended. This is undoubtedly the most inclusive reference that is available on Black Hills mammals. There are many publications, too numerous to mention, that deal with a specific group or individual species in the Black Hills. There are also many general references on mammals that cover a much broader area. However, Turner's excellent monograph relates specifically to this region and is, therefore, of great value to the mammalogist or general student interested in the Black Hills. The following checklist corresponds with the more complete, descriptive, accounts of species list published in Turner's monograph.

CHECKLIST OF MAMMALS OF THE BLACK HILLS

ORDER INSECTIVORA—Insectivores

Family SORICIDAE—Shrews

Masked Shrew   *Sorex cinereus haydeni* Baird

ORDER CHIROPTERA—Bats

Family VESPERTILIONIDAE—Vespertilionids

Keen's Myotis   *Myotis keenii septentrionalis* Trouessart
Small-footed Myotis   *Myotis leibii ciliolabrum* Merriam
Little Brown Myotis   *Myotis lucifugus carissima* Thomas
Fringe-tailed Myotis   *Myotis thysanodes pahasapensis* Jones and
                                       Genoways
Long-legged Myotis   *Myotis volans interior* Miller
Silver-haired Bat   *Lasionycteris noctivagans* Le Conte
Big Brown Bat   *Eptesicus fuscus pallidus* Young
Red Bat   *Lasiurus borealis borealis* Muller
Hoary Bat   *Lasiurus cinereus cinereus* Palisot de
                                       Beauvois
Townsend's Big-eared Bat   *Plecotus townsendii pallescens* Miller

ORDER LAGOMORPHA—Hares, Rabbits and Pikas

Family LEPORIDAE—Hares and Rabbits

Desert Cottontail   *Sylvilagus audubonii baileyi* Merriam

*Turner, Ronald W. 1974. *Mammals of the Black Hills of South Dakota and Wyoming.* Miscell. Publ. No. 60. University of Kansas Museum of Natural History, Lawrence, Kansas. 178 pp. (Ph.D. dissertation).

Eastern Cottontail	*Sylvilagus floridanus similis* Nelson
Nuttall's Cottontail	*Sylvilagus nuttallii grangeri* J. A. Allen
White-tailed Jack Rabbit	*Lepus townsendii campanius* Hollister

ORDER RODENTIA—Rodents

Family SCIURIDAE—Squirrels and Allies

Least Chipmunk	*Eutamias minimus pallidus* J. A. Allen
Least Chipmunk	*Eutamias minimus silvaticus* White
Yellow-bellied Marmot	*Marmota flaviventris dacota* Merriam
Thirteen-lined Ground Squirrel	*Spermophilus tridecemlineatus pallidus* J. A. Allen
Black-tailed Prairie Dog	*Cynomys ludovicianus ludovicianus* Ord
Fox Squirrel	*Sciurus niger rufiventer* E. Geoffroy St. Hilaire
Red Squirrel	*Tamiasciurus hudsonicus dakotensis* J. A. Allen
Northern Flying Squirrel	*Glaucomys sabrinus bangsi* Rhoads

Family GEOMYIDAE—Pocket Gophers

Northern Pocket Gopher	*Thomomys talpoides nebulosis* V. Bailey

Family HETEROMYIDAE—Pocket Mice and Kangaroo Rats

Olive-backed Pocket Mouse	*Perognathus fasciatus olivaceogriseus* Swenk
Hispid Pocket Mouse	*Perognathus hispidus paradoxus* Merriam
Ord's Kangaroo Rat	*Dipodomys ordii luteolus* Goldman
Ord's Kangaroo Rat	*Dipodomys ordii terrosus* Hoffmeister

Family CASTORIDAE—Beaver

Beaver	*Castor canadensis missouriensis* Bailey

Family CRICETIDAE—Native Rats, Mice and Voles

Western Harvest Mouse	*Reithrodontomys megalotis dychei* J. A. Allen
White-footed Mouse	*Peromyscus leucopus aridulus* Osgood
Deer Mouse	*Peromyscus maniculatus nebrascensis* Coues
Bushy-tailed Woodrat	*Neotoma cinerea orolestes* Merriam
Red-backed Vole	*Clethrionomys gapperi brevicaudus* Merriam
Long-tailed Vole	*Microtus longicaudus longicaudus* Merriam
Prairie Vole	*Microtus ochrogaster haydenii* Baird
Meadow Vole	*Microtus pennsylvanicus insperatus* J. A. Allen
Muskrat	*Ondatra zibethicus cinnamominus* Hollister

Family MURIDAE—Old World Rats and Mice

Norway Rat	*Rattus norvegicus* Berkenhout
House Mouse	*Mus musculus* Linnaeus

Family ZAPODIDAE—Jumping Mice

Meadow Jumping Mouse	*Zapus hudsonius campestris* Preble

Family ERETHIZONIDAE—Porcupines

Porcupine	*Erethizon dorsatum bruneri* Swenk

ORDER CARNIVORA—Carnivores

Family CANIDAE—Coyotes, Wolves and Foxes

Coyote	*Canis latrans latrans* Say
Gray Wolf*	*Canis lupus irremotus* Goldman
Red Fox	*Vulpes vulpes regalis* Merriam

Family URSIDAE—Bears

Black Bear	*Ursus americanus americanus* Pallas
Grizzly Bear*	*Ursus arctos horribilis* Ord

Family PROCYONIDAE—Raccoons

Raccoon	*Procyon lotor hirtus* Nelson and Goldman

Family MUSTELIDAE—Weasels, Skunks and Allies

Ermine	*Mustela erminea muricus* Bangs
Long-tailed Weasel	*Mustela frenata alleni* Merriam
Black-footed Ferret	*Mustela nigripes* Audubon and Bachman
Mink	*Mustela vison letifera* Hollister
Badger	*Taxidea taxus taxus* Schreber
Striped Skunk	*Mephitis mephitis husonica* Richardson

Family FELIDAE—Cats

Mountain Lion	*Felis concolor hippolestes* Merriam
Lynx	*Lynx canadensis canadensis* Kerr
Bobcat	*Lynx rufus pallescens* Merriam

ORDER ARTIODACTYLA—Even-toed Ungulates

Family CERVIDAE—Wapiti, Deer and Allies

Wapiti	*Cervus canadensis canadensis* Erxleben
Mule Deer	*Odocoileus hemionus hemionus* Rafinesque
White-tailed Deer	*Odocoileus virginianus dacotensis* Goldman and Kellogg

Family ANTILOCAPRIDAE—Pronghorn

Pronghorn	*Antilocapra americana americana* Ord

*Extinct in the Black Hills.

148

Family BOVIDAE—Bison, Sheep and Goats

Bison	*Bison bison bison* Linnaeus
Mountain Goat	*Oreamnos americanus missoulae* J. A. Allen
Mountain Sheep	*Ovis canadensis auduboni* Merriam

Existence of Following Species Questionable:

Opossum	*Didelphis marsupialis virginiana* Kerr
Dwarf Shrew	*Sorex namus* Merriam
Banded Bat	*Myotis grisescens* A. H. Howell
Spotted Bat	*Euderma maculatum* J. A. Allen
Snowshoe Hare	*Lepus americanus seclusus* Baker and Hankins
Black-tailed Jack Rabbit	*Lepus californicus melanotis* Mearns
Ground Squirrel	*Spermophilus spilosoma obsoletus* Kennicott
Silky Pocket Mouse	*Perognathus flavus piperi* Goldman
Plains Harvest Mouse	*Reithrodontomys montanus albescens* Cary
Northern Grasshopper Mouse	*Onychomys leucogaster arcticeps* Hollister
Sagebrush Vole	*Lagurus curtatus levidensis* Goldman
Swift Fox	*Vulpes velox hebes* Merriam
Gray Fox	*Urocyon cinereoargenteus ocythous* Bangs
Spotted Skunk	*Spilogale putorius interrupta* Rafinesque
* Pine Marten	*Martes americana vulpina* Rafinesque
** Fisher	*Martes pennanti pennanti* Erxleben
Wolverine	*Gulo gulo luscus* Linnaeus
Otter	*Lutra canadensis canadensis* Schreber
Fallow Deer	*Dama dama* Linnaeus

*The last recorded pine marten was taken in the Black Hills in 1930, west of Custer. Beginning in 1979 a re-introduction program was established by the South Dakota Department of Game, Fish and Parks, in cooperation with the Western South Dakota Fur Harvesters and the South Dakota Trappers Association. To date 72 martens have been released in suitable habitat in the northern and central Hills, with plans to release 50 more animals in the next two year. Marten appear to be increasing naturally in the Hills, indicating a recovery of a once native species.

**There is some evidence that the Fisher does exist in the Hills. Two specimens have been accidentally taken in the Hills proper during the past decade. The Fisher is a very secretive animal, and if remnant populations do exist here, it is not known where. There have been suggestions of a reintroduction plan, but nothing has been formally done.

149

Part IV
CURRENT ENVIRONMENT OF THE HILLS

INTRODUCTION

The viewpoints expressed in this section are personal and are admittedly slanted toward an overall ecological and environmental protection perspective. Before it is too late more people must become involved in representing the flora and fauna, the water and soil, the clean air and tranquility that have been characteristic of the Black Hills. I am a professional biologist, albeit retired, and observe things from that point of view. I undoubtedly see effects and potential effects of change that others may not see, simply because of background training and experience.

My comments are based upon the experience of over 35 years of research and observations with the conclusions resulting from such studies. During this time I have lived in the Hills a substantial part of each year and have traveled extensively throughout the area. This has afforded me the opportunity to closely observe environmental trends and changes in the Hills. Sometimes the changes have been subtle and gradual, at other times rapid and spectacular, dependent of course, upon the situation and the factors that are changing.

I readily admit that there are other points of view and that economic factors must be considered...people must be allowed to make a living. Also, the agencies that establish policy and are in management situations are forced by local, state and federal governments to operate on a fiscally sound basis. The effect of such restrictions makes decision making that much more difficult.

However, I feel strongly that, at the present time and during the past two decades in particular, fewer people have seriously represented the preservationist point of view than the economic factor. The decisions that have been made in the past have reflected this, with the result that the dramatic changes in the Hills environment herein discussed have occurred. Most of the changes affecting the overall environment of the area have been the direct result of compromises between economic development forces and preservation agencies. The issues are clear to the advocates of each opposing group ...unfortunately, the solutions are usually short-term, and do not consider the long-range impact on the environment of the Hills.

150

An immediate "band-aid" solution that appears to satisfy both points of view may be politically expedient. However, we can no longer afford such compromises. In a critical, relatively small ecosystem such as the Black Hills, one dominant and simple fact must be clearly understood by all. There will be no economic development in the future without a healthy environment. The economy of the Hills is completely dependent upon the environment. For example, without water nothing survives. The mining, agriculture, logging and tourism industries, as well as every living being, are totally dependent upon an adequate, uncontaminated water supply. This fact, alone, defies compromise.

It ultimately boils down to this: (1) should a biologically, geologically and historically unique area...the Black Hills...be preserved in a condition as near as possible to its current state for the overall benefit of present and future generations, or, (2) should the region be continually exploited for short-term economic reasons and probably be changed irreparably, if not destroyed?

Since the majority of the area is the *Black Hills National Forest*, and has been since February 22, 1897, when President Cleveland established it by proclamation, and therefore owned by the people of the United States, shouldn't management policies be based on that fact, thus relegating economic gains for relatively few individuals and corporations to secondary consideration?

Hard questions concerning the Black Hills must be addressed soon, or it will be too late. As with any controversial issue, each side is convinced it is right and that there really is no reason to change policy or place restrictions on activities. "It's been like this for 100 years and we have survived...the Hills are still here...so why change now?"

Such simple-minded reasoning is strongly suggestive of the old theme of Manifest Destiny and fails to recognize that areas such as the Black Hills, or the entire continent for that matter, are finite. The ultimate question seems to be, "what does it take to convince enough people, once and for all, that we are running out of resources and unique areas such as our Black Hills?"

BACKGROUND

The Black Hills area is, undoubtedly, South Dakota's, as well as one of the Nation's, greatest natural resources. As such, the area should be preserved as nearly as possible to its present state if a reasonable stewardship of its natural beauty and remaining resources is to be practiced. Nowhere else on the continent can be found an area of such diversity within such a relatively restricted space.

The fact that the Hills are a relatively small, isolated upthrust surrounded by high, dry plains, means that the environment is very fragile, at best. As a result, changes become critical and more pronounced than in larger, more uniform, ecosystems. Moreover, what may appear to be minor or subtle changes at the present time, often have an impact that results in much greater changes and environmental problems over a period of time. Thus, changes in the Hills environment, particularly those that are the result of human activities, must be carefully monitored and revised whenever possible.

Historically, the majority of the land within the Black Hills is National Forest land and is, therefore, managed by the U.S. Forest Service. The Service has operated under original guidelines and policies established "for the long term use and enjoyment of the American people." The principles of multiple use and sustained yield have been the major guidelines in management policy. According to official publications, these principles "seek to assure that the Black Hills National Forest will continue to produce a multitude of forest products and services to meet the needs of the people of South Dakota and the nation."

Private interests, corporations and individuals, also own a large proportion of the Black Hills land area. Control of these lands rests, of course, with the owners. These tracts were for the most part acquired as the result of the Homestead act and mining claims in the late 1800's. The majority of the private lands are surrounded by the forest, therefore, general total management of the Black Hills is complex.

Private interests and Forest Service policy sometimes are in conflict. The Forest Service suggests general guidelines and has authority to enforce them, such as fire control measures, or access to private property through government land. However, the land owner has ba-

152

sic control and jurisdiction over his property. This has resulted in serious environmental problems, particularly in the Northern Hills, when the overall Black Hills environment is considered.

"From the time of its establishment, the Forest Service administered the Black Hills forests so as to meet the economic need of the mining and industrial interests of the region. The forests have been managed on a sustained yield basis to produce a perpetual supply of timber for mines and mills. Grazing, wildlife, recreational and other activities are integrated with the more important timber activity so that each is given the relative importance to which it is entitled."*

This policy has basically continued to the present time. As a result of large sections of the forest deteriorating, in 1970 a new concept known as Area Management Planning (AMP) was implemented by the forest service in the attempt to improve specific areas. In 1972, Kenneth Scholz, BHNF supervisor, stated: "New springs, improved food area use patterns by deer, growth of aspen in selected fuel break areas for fire protection or a colorful fall view, and logging with the view in mind that scarcely changes the appearance of a mountainside are developments noted even now in the AMP."

However, conditions did not improve under this type of management. Further degradation of the forests and the general environment persists.

During the 1980's, Land and Resource Management Plans were introduced that require the forest supervisor to review the conditions on the land covered every five years to determine whether conditions or demands of the public have changed significantly. A five year evaluation of the Black Hills National Forest Plan for 1984-1988 was prepared in October 1989. This evaluation, coupled with a new five year management plan to be released in 1990, hopefully will provide essential data and information upon which the forest service will be able to improve environmental conditions throughout the Black Hills.

The first operational plan directed that the forests be managed so as to "maintain harmony among all the major activities associated with the forest including mining, timber harvest, grazing, tourism and recreation, with priority given to the first three."

Meanwhile many individuals, and environmental agencies, particularly in the 1980's, have become alarmed over the deteriorating con-

*Official map, Black Hills and Harney National Forest, 1940, U.S.D.A., Forest Service.

153

dition of the Hills and have advocated restrictions and changed policies to thwart further destruction of the Hills total environment. Most of these efforts have been directed toward public interest and awareness of private corporation activities involving mining in the Northern Hills and waste disposal operations in the Edgemont area, south of the Hills proper. Throughout the Hills water resources, road construction, overgrazing, timber management and wildlife, have also been targeted as critical and involve both private and forest service land. These concerns are the topics more thoroughly discussed below.

CURRENT ENVIRONMENTAL CONCERNS

The following problems in the overall ecology of the Hills must be addressed and solved in future management plans if the area is to recover and sustain its uniqueness and beauty.

WATER

During the past decade the most significant change in the general environment of the Hills has been the precipitous decline in water resources. The water level of lakes and streams have exhibited a spectacular decline, but of even more significance is the lowering of the water table generally. Surface and underground water supplies have reached the critical stage throughout the Hills. Ironically, surface and ground water are closely inter-related here. The limestone formation springs pump ground water to the surface and a portion seeps back into the ground. Some of the streams actually go underground for some distance before emerging again to the surface (ex-Spearfish Creek). Obviously annual cycles of precipitation effect the recharging of ground water.

The severe drought of the late 1980's, obviously, is a major contributing factor to the water problem, but it is by no means the total cause. There has been a continuing downward trend in both surface and groundwater levels for many years. When, and if, the drought breaks there will still continue to be water problems.

Many factors are involved which collectively are responsible for the water loss: (1) Pine forests have become much too thick, a fact that can be easily documented by comparative photographs of the same area taken at widely spaced time intervals. Over the past 100 years there has been a spectacular increase in the pine population with widespread, stagnated young stands that are grossly overcrowded and unproductive (dog-haired pine). Large volumes of water are consumed daily by the pine forests of the Hills. (2) Overgrazing by cattle and wildlife, particularly in headwaters areas, have resulted in compaction of the soil around springs, resulting in much reduced stream flow. (3) With stream flow reduced riparian (streamside) vegetation has been drastically reduced. (4) With no water available in the streams and no young trees and shrubs upon which to feed, beaver populations have decreased markedly, hence no small dams acting as holding ponds for water. (5) Large volumes of water are required for the operation of industries, particularly mining. (6) Increasing demands for more water by agricultural interests, both for irrigation and grazing cattle. (7) A sharp increase in housing developments has occurred during the 1980's which require more private wells. (8) Growth of demands for water in towns and cities, with unfortunately, no accompanying significant water restrictions (lawns, pools, golf courses, etc.).

Pactola Reservoir, August 1989. Photo by author.

155

All of these factors, collectively, impose a tremendously large burden on natural water supplies. When added to long-term drought, it becomes readily apparent that water availability is the most critical environmental factor in the Black Hills. In fact, reserve water supplies that have been held in major reservoirs have dropped to extremely serious levels. By the end of August, 1989, Pactola Reservoir dropped to a surface level 45 feet below the normal conservation level.

PONDEROSA PINE FOREST

The Black Hills ecosystem is rapidly becoming a climax forest. This means ecologically that the dominant species (Pinus ponderosa Laws,) is becoming stable and is perpetuating itself and driving other species out. The Hills are moving toward a pine-grassland community to the exclusion of other once prominent species (trees, shrubs, and forbs). The climate and soils of the area are well suited to pine and natural ecological succession is running its course to the pine climax.

The "Smokey Bear" concept of fire control plus current policies of forest management are major reasons for the increase in the pine forests. Controlled burning and intensified thinning are needed to reduce the pine population. Although logging operations have been an on-going operational concept for years, the overall thinning effect, although helpful, has not been sufficiently effective. Most logging operations take only marketable pine because of cost effectiveness. Dog-haired stands are not thinned, or eliminated.

Natural selection involves periodic "opening" of the forest as a result of fires, destructive winds, insects or other factors, but this natural control process requires long periods of time.

Therefore, unless natural phenomena occur, or stringent control measures taken, the climax forest persists. When dog-haired stands are present only one third of the moisture that falls gets to the ground. This has an extremely detrimental effect on water sources. Such overcrowding prevents penetration of sunlight, thus driving forbs and grasses out. This, in turn, means lack of cover and food for wildlife. Overcrowding also stunts the trees so that they do not reach marketable size. Moreover, fire hazards are increased for "hot fires" which destroy all the ground cover.

156

Typical dog-haired pine. Photo by author, 1989.

The essential ingredient that has been missing in past forest management is maintaining the Hills capacity to produce grasses, wildflowers, shrubs and trees, in addition to pine. That is what must be kept uppermost in the minds of future public and private land managers...the difference between exploitation and careful husbandry. A forest no longer abused will slowly regain the productivity ultimately determined by the soil, climate and the biological capacities of its natural components.

LAKES

The drought of the past few years has, obviously, been the major factor in the current condition of the lakes. The major reservoirs have suffered the most, not only because of lack of water to maintain water levels, but drawdown for city water supplies and irrigation have greatly exceeded intake. The smaller lakes have fared better and have maintained reasonable levels. Some have suffered severe siltation problems (Stockade Lake is currently being treated by extensive dredging.) Aquatic vegetation is increasing markedly in many of the lakes prob-

157

Deerfield Lake. Photo by author, August 1989.

ably caused by increased nitrates drawn in from the watershed. Long term ecological succession is operative here as elsewhere.

Fish populations of the lakes have remained good to excellent, largely due to the restocking program of the South Dakota Game, Fish and Parks Department. Stream fishing has dropped considerably in recent years because of the low water levels of most of the streams. In those streams where the waterflow is still adequate, reasonably good trout fishing has been maintained.

STREAMS AND ASSOCIATED RIPARIAN ZONES

When the advanced stages of a pine forest climax are reached other once-present species can no longer compete. In the Hills the result has been that a once lush riparian (streamside) vegetation which was so characteristic is rapidly disappearing in the majority of the drainages. Once consisting of a heavy deciduous mixture of several species of willow, dogwood, paper and river birch, wildrose, forbs, sedges, grasses, etc., it is now rare to encounter these complexes. The vegetation of many streamsides and floodplains now is dominated by

158

grasses with little, if any, shrub zone.

The dominant pine forest is not the only cause of this condition, however. Overgrazing, haying, clearing of the valleys by burning, spraying and grubbing out trees and shrubs all have taken their toll. This is particularly true on private lands. Unfortunately, a large portion of the valleys and drainages of the Hills are in private ownership. Apparently top priority has been given to managing for timber and grasslands.

Streams and their associated riparian zones are extremely important in the Black Hills, being the lifeline for trout fisheries, and supplying water for domestic, recreational, and agricultural uses. Historically riparian ecosystems have been, biologically, the most productive communities in the Hills. These areas provide critical habitat for wildlife, mostly due to the extensive edge and diversity created by more moist conditions surrounded by dry upland. They are also valuable in maintaining stability for stream channels, and water quality protection.

Because of a lack of sufficient current data, and in view of the obviously deteriorating condition of streams and riparian zones a comprehensive study was initiated in the Black Hills in 1984. This project, *Inventory and Classification of Black Hills Streams and Riparian Areas*, was a cooperative effort of a number of agencies due to the resources required and the complex nature of the study. These agencies included the Black Hills National Forest, South Dakota Department of Game, Fish and Parks, the Department of Water and Natural Resources, South Dakota State University, and the Rocky Mountain Forest and Range Experiment Station.

The stated objective of the study was "to develop a vegetation inventory of all riparian areas." The report, completed in 1985, is the first step in evaluating Black Hills riparian vegetation. The importance of riparian systems to the overall environment of the Hills is clearly stated in the introduction to the report: "the health of a riparian system is to a large degree dependent on the condition of the vegetative community. Well-developed riparian vegetation provides wildlife with nesting sites, cover, forage, and corridors for migrations and movements. Fish also require a good streamside vegetation component for overhead cover, instream temperature moderation, terrestrial insects, stream recharge from stored ground water, and filtering sedi-

159

ment movement into the stream. Riparian vegetation is susceptible to degradation from land use activities (e.g. livestock grazing, roads, recreation, development) that, unfortunately, tend to be concentrated along streams. In order to properly deal with these areas managers need to know the current vegetation composition and how it relates to the site's potential."

A subsequent study will evaluate potential natural communities, associated seral states and directional trends. It is imperative that proper attention be given to riparian areas, and hopefully, the agencies that sponsored the study will follow through and take the necessary action to insure that these vital biological communities are protected from further deterioration and attempt to restore them to a healthy condition.

Riparian vegetation in poor condition along Castle Creek. Photo by author, 1989.

WILDLIFE

The current status of bird and mammal populations in the Hills appears to reflect somewhat different trends. Whereas bird populations seem to have remained relatively stable, there have been definite changes in the population density of a number of mammals. Reasons for this are not clear other than it may reflect the superior migratory capacity of birds.

160

BIRDS

The only reliable long range information of Black Hills bird populations are the records of the annual Breeding Bird Surveys program of the United States Fish and Wildlife Service. Since 1967, Dr. Nathaniel Whitney, of Rapid City, has conducted these annual surveys for two major routes in the Black Hills. His records reveal no dramatic changes for the common and abundant regularly occurring species. Variations in numbers for a species over the years appear to be within the range of normal cycles.

Recent *South Dakota Bird Notes* records indicate that the Pigmy Nuthatch, Cassin's Finch, and House Finch have been added to the list of permanent residents. Also noted is an increase, since 1983, of reports of sightings of Clark's Nutcracker (significant numbers were reported in the central and southern Hills during the winter of 1986-87, with two active nests verified in Custer County during April, 1987).

MAMMALS

The mammals discussed here were selected because of their changed status during the late 1970's and 1980's. Such changes are prime indicators of serious habitat problems for many native species. Availability of food, water, and cover are, obviously, the key factors in maintaining healthy animal populations. In a relatively restricted area such as the Black Hills, the precarious balance of nature is easily upset. What the future holds for the wildlife of the Hills will be largely determined by decisions made within the next few years.

With some exceptions, population densities of most of the small mammals do not appear to have changed significantly, other than the typical cycles they experience. The prairie dog became very abundant in the southern hills during the early 1980's. Control efforts were necessary and numbers were significantly reduced, but they are currently on the rise once again. Marmot, badger, porcupine and bobcat populations have declined, whereas racoon populations have increased significantly throughout the entire state, including the Hills.

Beaver

Beaver numbers have decreased markedly in all areas of the Black Hills that once held beaver colonies, largely due to two factors: (1)

161

Dry beaver dams on Negro Creek. Photo by author, 1989.

The extended drought has drastically reduced stream flow, with many completely dry; (2) overgrazing of bottomlands by cattle, and because of the drought, some wildlife. This has prohibited willow, aspen, birch, cottonwood and other shrubs and trees from re-establishing growth. Without their food source and no water, beaver cannot sur-

Adult beaver. Photo courtesy Deb Waite, 1989.

vive. In those few remaining areas that can support beaver colonies, the Game, Fish and Parks Department, in cooperation with the Forest Service, is currently transplanting beaver into them. These transplants have been very successful in establishing mature colonies, particularly in the Norbeck Wildlife Preserve and the Black Elk Wilderness, but also in other areas. However, in the major part of the Hills, the forest is rapidly approaching the climax stage and beaver cannot survive in a dominant ponderosa pine forest.

Coyote

Since the 1970's coyote numbers have dramatically increased in the Hills, as well as throughout South Dakota. This is undoubtedly due to the fact that control measures (use of toxicants) for the coyote population were discontinued, bounties lifted, and fur prices tumbled. The coyote is a very adaptable animal and has currently invaded every possible niche within the Black Hills. The saturation point for this species is approaching rapidly. Numbers will probably fluctuate little in the near future.

Black Bear

Reports of black bear activity continue to occur. The most recent report came from the Castle Creek area west of Deerfield lake, in the fall of 1989. In spite of these occasional reports, the black bear is still considered a rare species in the Hills.

Mountain Lion
(Cougar, Puma, Panther, Catamount)

One of the most interesting changes in animal populations within the Black Hills has been a decided increase in mountain lion activity. For many years there have been numerous reports of the presence of mountain lions in the Hills, but most of them were not officially verified. As a result of these reports, in the fall of 1985, Ted Benzon, wildlife biologist with the South Dakota Department of Game, Fish, and Parks, initiated a study of all documented sightings or tracks. Since that time he has documented 84 actual sightings, measured

163

tracks, and mapped mountain lion distribution for the Black Hills area. In addition he has recorded numerous accounts of lions that were unable to be substantiated and therefore could not be included in these figures.

However, a creditable population estimate, and/or sex and age ratios, is extremely difficult to predict, due to the lack of proper data and the broad home range and territory generally covered by a single individual lion.

Although the most frequent reports have come from the central and southern hills, reports have come from throughout the hills.

Prior to the turn of the century, mountain lions were considered to be numerous in the Black Hills. In the early 1900's, as with so many of the large game animals, the population steadily decreased to the point where, for some time, it was generally thought to be extinct in the Hills. Largely due to its solitary habits and "cunning lifestyle", most outdoor enthusiasts never see one, or are unaware of their presence.

Due to the large number of undocumented reports and the number that have been authenticated by professionals, it is safe to state unequivocally that the mountain lion currently exists in the Hills. Moreover, the population has increased markedly during the last decade, particularly in the southern hills. Ted Benzon states: "the big cat has been with us for many years."

Deer

When wildlife populations are discussed, undoubtedly deer, both white-tail and mule, more than any other animal, attract the interest of most people. This is particularly true in the Black Hills. . ."deer and the Hills are practically synonymous."

The following summary clearly reflects the current and future status of deer populations in the Black Hills under current forest conditions and management. It was prepared by Leslie Rice, big game biologist, of the Division of Wildlife, South Dakota Department of Game, Fish and Parks.

"Twenty year trends in Black Hills deer herds have been steadily downward. Yearly fluctuations have occurred but long term herd status has been in decline. Causative factors are many. Historic winter ranges on private lands were located on ranches dominated by riparian and meadows complex habitats. Housing developments expanding from metropolitan areas have substantially reduced availability of these historic ranges. With housing developments, human related disturbance has also increased.

Decrease in private land habitat availability has forced big game herds to utilize historic ranges on United States National Forest lands to a greater degree. Unfortunately, elimination of natural fires has caused plant successional stages to favor ponderosa pine plant communities. As successional stages approach climax vegetation, desirable forage and habitat types favoring deer herds have substantially been reduced. Forbs, shrubs and deciduous tree habitat types are steadily declining with fire elimination. This has forced conflicts among those forest uses mandated by multiple-use management. Timber industry and domestic livestock uses are in direct conflict with big game habitat requirements. Priority levels are such that deer herds have suffered.

Future conflicts will arise between deer habitat needs and economic development throughout the Black Hills. Mining industry, tourism, recreation and a host of other factors all will negatively influence deer numbers now and in the future. The next twenty years will undoubtedly see further decreases in deer numbers under present society mandated priorities."

INSECT DAMAGE

Foresters have become concerned about the mountain pine beetle (Dendroctonus ponderosae Hopk.) which became a serious problem in the 1980's with areas of infestation widespread throughout the Hills. Apparently it has declined slightly in recent years. An active program of control has been in effect during the past 5 years, largely involving thinning operations. Thin stands of pine are less likely to become infected. Dense, homogeneous stands, particularly trees 8-12 inches in diameter, are most susceptible to the beetle. Individual and clustered "bug trees" can readily be detected from a distance by their brown color. Dead trees should be cut and burned to help decrease spreading the infestation.

With recent drought conditions ('86-'89), there has been a notable increase in the population of another beetle (several species of the genus Ips). However, Forest Service officials do not consider this insect to be a problem at the present time.

GRAZING

Historically, in keeping with management policies that assign high priority to cattle grazing, the Forest Service has granted permits for grazing allotments throughout the Black Hills. Such allotments are based on a specified number of cattle permitted seasonally on a given range unit.

Heavy livestock use of the National Forest is of deep concern to the general public and a major issue with the South Dakota Department of Game, Fish and Parks. Conflicts between grazing and other activities has been increasing and will become more intense as more people establish homes here or come to the Hills for recreational purposes.

Cattle grazing "anywhere in the Hills".
Photo by author, 1989.

A major objective of the 1980's Forest Operating Plan was to sustain the current permitted grazing use while at the same time maintain satisfactory range conditions. Obviously, this was not workable,

166

particularly under severe drought conditions. Moreover, budget allocations of the Forest Service have not been adequate to implement needed improvement in management.

In the attempt to analyze range conditions, during the time period 1984-89, the Forest Service surveyed 29 grazing allotments on non-forested National Forest lands. Only open areas were considered meaningful since they most closely reflect ecological conditions. This survey revealed that only 52% of the acres surveyed were classified as satisfactory, with 48% in unsatisfactory range condition and requiring corrective measures.

In addition, of course, a large proportion of the non-forested, open meadows and valleys are privately owned and the landowner controls

Typical hayed meadow. Photo by author, 1989.

haying and grazing operations. Both on federal and private lands, particularly near springs and streams, overgrazing has resulted in unsatisfactory range conditions in many areas.

The issue is being faced and some progress is being made, in some Forest Districts, using different management systems. Practices such as fencing of riparian areas and more fencing for better livestock distribution are also being applied on some allotments, but not others. More uniform application of these management practices is needed.

167

The multiple use concept of forest lands must also be recognized and applied by restricting certain areas from cattle grazing. This is particularly important in heavily used recreational areas such as campgrounds, streams and lakes.

Under open range conditions, it is, admittedly, difficult to control numbers and distribution of cattle. Hopefully, in the 1990's management budgets will be increased so as to allow adequate monitoring of cattle and surveying of range conditions on a regular basis.

WASTE DISPOSAL

For many years waste disposal has been an issue that has generated heated controversy, particularly in regard to the Edgemont area, on the southwest edge of the Hills. Although not in the Hills proper, the area in question is sufficiently close to warrant major concerns on the part of environmentalists. In this case economic gains versus environmental contamination have caused sharp public reaction for, and against, attempts to convert former United States Government Ordinance Depot land and facilities (operated from the 1940's to the 1960's) to disposal sites for hazardous and solid wastes.

During the 1980's several proposals were submitted to the South Dakota Board of Minerals and Environment for the importation of hazardous and solid wastes, ultimately to be stored in the old depot area. Ironically, the sponsoring agencies were all out-of-state groups. Fortunately, public reaction forced the rejection of a proposal for a dump for low-level nuclear wastes.

In the mid 80's a permit to store imported sewage ash was issued to Consolidated Management Corporation. Legal complications have resulted from this agreement as a result of failure to comply with regulations, but sewage ash is currently stockpiled in the Igloo-Provo area. In September of 1989 a permit was issued to South Dakota Disposal Systems, Golden, Colorado, to store solid wastes. This was a one year permit limited to burying 300,000 tons of garbage, with future plans in line for up to one million tons per year. This project is also in litigation currently.

MINING

In the 1980's the environmental change that has precipitated the most publicity and public debate is undoubtedly the mining issue, particularly surface mining (open-pit and strip mining) for gold in the Northern Hills.

The 1872 Mining Act permits mineral development on National Forest lands "in an orderly fashion through Forest Service approved operating plans, with timely and effective rehabilitation required for disturbed lands. Reclamation emphasizes restoration similar to existing scenic values of landform and vegetative characteristics." District Rangers are responsible for monitoring mining operations in their respective districts. Unfortunately the Forest Service operation plan for the 1980's did not address large scale surface mines. While attention recently has been focused on the Northern Hills, due to increased activity in surface and open pit mining, uranium mining in the southern Hills, an important issue in the 1970's and early 1980's, has become almost a non-issue.

In 1986 the Forest Service operating plan was modified to include two documents pertaining to minerals: (1) United States Geological Survey Publication 1580, *Mineral Resource Potential and Geology of the Black Hills National Forest;* (2) *Best Minerals Management Practices: a Guide to Resource Management and Reclamation of Mined Lands in the Black Hills of South Dakota and Wyoming.*

New State of South Dakota mineral policy should result from two recently passed laws. *The Centennial Environmental Protection Act* of 1989 calls for a study of the cumulative effects of mining in the Black Hills. *The Special and Unique Lands Act* of 1989 recommends protection of special areas in the Black Hills. Mining in the Black Hills was the subject of an initiative on the South Dakota ballot, November 1989. The issue continues to be highly controversial and of widespread state, regional and national interest. A major factor of the mining issue is whether large open-pit mines or strip mines should be allowed at all, or whether the size of the operation should be limited on forest service lands.

Currently, 24 companies are either exploring or actively mining in the Black Hills. Ironically, all but one are from out of state or out of the United States. The total area now under permit or permit application in the Hills is in excess of 23 square miles. In addition, ap-

169

Homestake Open Pit Mine, Lead.
Photo by author, 1989.

proximately 28% of the Hills or 571,200 acres, were under active exploration as of 1988.

Surface mining on the scale being practiced in the Black Hills is relatively new to South Dakota. With the exception of the Homestake open pit mine in Lead which dates back to the gold rush days of 1876*, surface mining was not considered cost effective until the 1980's when the price of gold increased spectacularly. In addition, by that time, huge earth moving machines and equipment were available and new technology once more made it profitable to mine low grades of gold ore.

The new process is called heap-leaching. The surface material is first removed to reach the gold-bearing ore. The ore is blasted and ground to gravel size, then heaped up over huge piles of clay and plastic pad beds. The heap is sprayed with a cyanide solution that leaches through the ore and separates out the metals. This solution is conveyed to a holding pond and then to a mill where the metals are removed. The cyanide is recycled over the heap until no more metal leaches out. The waste ore is disposed as tailings and new ore piled on the pads to continue the process.

*Note: Although surface-mined initially and going underground early, the Homestake open pit was active from 1925-1942, closed down during World War II, re-opened briefly in 1947, but abandoned because the price of gold did not warrant the costs of extraction.

170

Surface mining, east slope of Terry Peak.
Photo by author, 1989.

With activities of the magnitude of current, let alone future, surface mining operations in the Hills, it is obvious that major environmental changes must be anticipated. Decisions now being made are critical to both the mining industry and to the future of the Black Hills.

Environmentalists anticipate problems from proposals such as these reported in the newsletter of the Technical Information Project, Rapid City, February 6, 1989:

> (1) Brohm Mining Corporation and the U.S. Forest Service signed a "Collection Agreement" in December 1988 in which Brohm agrees to pay for an Environmental Impact Study (EIS) to be conducted by the Forest Service. The EIS will begin as soon as Brohm submits a "Plan of Operations" detailing their proposed sulfide expansion.
>
> Brohm's proposed expansion will entail:
> (a) Use of 800 acres of federal land in the Galena area of the Black Hills National Forest.
> (b) An open pit that will reportedly be three times the size of Homestake's Open Cut.
> (c) A major tailings impoundment likely to be located in Lost Gulch.

171

(d) Sulfide ore and tailings, which generate acid drainage high in heavy metals.

(e) A new mill to process the sulfide ores.

(f) Extensive water use from Bear Butte Creek and adjoining streams and aquifers.

The Governor's legislative proposal (1990) to limit permitted affected acreage for surface mining would halt Brohm's expansion until after completion of a cumulative EIS on mining in the Black Hills. The EIS to be conducted by the Forest Service for Brohm would presumably be a site-specific study to assess the impacts of Brohm's operation alone. Once Brohm submits a "Plan of Operations," the Forest Service must conduct "scoping hearings" to solicit public input on concerns that should be addressed by EIS.

(2) The state Water Management Board issued a groundwater variance and discharge permit to Golden Reward in July 1989, so the company could begin dumping spent ore at their Terry Peak site. Golden Reward asked for variances from state groundwater quality standards for arsenic, cadmium, nitrate, nitrite, fluoride, chloride, sulfate, total dissolved solids, and pH.

Currently, legislation is pending in the South Dakota legislature in regard to surface mining in the Black Hills. A moratorium on new mining, extending through 1991, was designed to give state agencies and lawmakers time to study the cumulative effects of the industry in the Black Hills and whether or not to strengthen state mining laws.

Major concerns of environmentalists, generally, are:

1. *Land disturbance*

Can large cuts really be reclaimed?

How do you restore a mountain?

How are huge deposits of tailings handled?

2. *Water*

Mining requires huge amounts of water. . .where will it come from?

What are the long-term effects of leaching on ground water?

Will surface water be contaminated by cyanide leaks, sulphuric acid, etc.?

3. *Fisheries and Wildlife*
What are the long-term effects on fish and wildlife?
How much habitat will be destroyed?

4. *National Forest Lands*
Should the mining industry be allowed to encroach on land owned by the people of the United States?

5. *Aesthetics*
Should we tolerate the conversion of a beautiful area to ugly rock piles?

Unfortunately, the track record of the mining interests in the Hills, in regard to concern for the environment, has been less than exemplary.

It took Homestake Mining Company more than 100 years before they finally succumbed to environmentalist's pressure, and enforcement of state laws, to clean up Whitewood Creek. This was perhaps the ugliest, most contaminated stream to be found anywhere, because of the minetailings from Homestake and the dumping of raw sewage into the creek by the city of Deadwood. Yet, the people of the area tolerated it in defense of economic factors.

This became "the ecological laughing stock" of the entire region. It is a classic example of "collective corporate unconcern" for the environment.

Finally, following years of research, development of new technology, and massive efforts on the part of many, Homestake Mining Company, the cities of Lead and Deadwood, with the help of federal grants, and at the expenditure of 40 million dollars, cleared Whitewood Creek. After more than 100 years an industrial and domestic sewer was reborn to become a healthy stream.

It undoubtedly will take strict laws, not emotional reactions on both sides of the issue, before the problem of surface mining in the Black Hills is resolved.

EPILOGUE
WHAT DOES THE FUTURE HOLD?

Making predictions is always a hazardous undertaking, and predicting the future of the Black Hills is no exception. Based on past his-

173

tory, it is relatively safe to assume that greater pressures than ever before will be exerted on the Hills by utilitarian interests on the one hand and by environmental partisans on the other. The combination of increased population and dwindling resources will take its toll on the Hills, as it has elsewhere on the continent. As the land base dwindles, increased controversy will undoubtedly arise over the use of public lands, and exploitation of private lands.

Cattlemen will continue to claim the Hills as a potential range resource worthy of intensive development and will demand more grazing leases and water development. Their critics will continue to lobby for preserving larger areas of the Hills in a natural state with fewer cattle grazing on National Forest lands.

Mining interests will continue to attempt to acquire more public lands for open-pit mining. Private lands will be further exploited for mining of a wide variety of rocks and minerals.

Water development is absolutely essential in order to meet the needs of towns, cities, new housing developments, industry and agriculture.

The logging industry will continually exert pressure for greatly expanded permits and leases for harvesting mature pine. This will result in continued pine forest management policies as a top priority.

Sportsmen will continue to demand more and better opportunities for hunting and fishing. Recreational interests will increase the demand for camping facilities, snowmobile routes, cross-country and downhill skiing opportunities and hiking and riding trails.

The tourism industry will continue to increase its efforts to provide more and better attractions. This will result in additional advertising billboards, tourist attractions along major highways, and pressure for better and newer road development. Such developments create distractions and reinforce the opinion of many that, in order to really appreciate the natural wonder and beauty of the Hills and Badlands, one must leave the highways and travel the backroads.

Proponents of waste disposal sites and their adversaries will continue to pursue their respective positions.

Recognizing that the Black Hills is so unique, environmental agencies such as the Surface Mining Initiative Fund, Technical Information Project, Citizens Against Destructive Mining, South Dakota Resources Coalition, Environmental Protection Agency, and the Sierra Club will increase their efforts to conserve and preserve this truly remarkable natural area.

It is now twenty years since the first Earth Day was organized. The concepts around which Earth Day was centered were all very well intentioned. Unfortunately the environmental problems that plague the earth have not only not been solved in the interim, the environment has continued to deteriorate steadily.

The clear message of Earth Day is that the capital wealth of the earth, the nation, South Dakota, or the Black Hills lies in our natural resources. We have been spending our capital at an alarming rate. Any agency that systematically expends its capital is ultimately doomed to disaster. It is as clear as that!

On the positive side, in the Black Hills, a fine example of what cooperative, informed effort can accomplish is the McIntosh Fen, located just west of Deerfield in the Castle Creek drainage. Here, the initial stages of a renewable recovery of riparian and floodplain vegetation reveal what can be done.

Hopefully the responsible agencies will continue to cooperatively move in this direction throughout the Black Hills. Human creativity is fully capable of finding acceptable solutions to any environmental problem. The question seems to persist. . .will current generations demand it?

Sven G. Froiland
The Limestone Bluffs
Custer, South Dakota
1990

175

Treasures of Solitude:
The Spirit of the Black Hills

A silent implosion of
inconceivable beauty.
The rare, the unique,
the sacred, the
powerful.
All alive within the
Spirit of the Hills.

Glistening gold.
A treasure of the earth.
Among the red soils of the Spearfish;
Scattered within the conifers of the Limestone Plateau;
Reflected in the glistening clear springs.

Within the whisper of the wind through
the Ponderosa . . .we seem to hear the fading lumbersome
footfalls of the mammoth,
a broken chant of a saddened Indian,
the listless moan of a wounded earth,
the heartbeat of nature.

As the wind sings through the pines,
the snowflakes of winter cascade
silently to this whitened earth
lightly covering, healing.

The pasque flower heralds the spring,
a living thread from ancient time and echoing footfalls.
The glorious energy of sun-driven life
warms summer trails.

And with the aspen-gold of autumn,
the heart soars with the joy, the beauty,
and the peace of the Hills.
Yet again, in the solitude of winter,
we know that it is time. . .
to touch the *Paha Sapa* with caring hands.

Paige Wolken and R. Weedon

176

Part V

THE BADLANDS

Ronald R. Weedon

INTRODUCTION

Some of the most spectacular scenery in all of the Great Plains is to be found in the *White River Badlands* of southwestern South Dakota. Called *Mako Sica (mako,* land; *sica,* bad) by the Sioux and *Les Mauvaises Terres a Traverser* (bad lands to travel across) by eighteenth century French-Canadian fur trappers, the area is starkly beautiful, peaceful and desolate with some of the most outstanding sunsets to be found anywhere. The term "badlands" generally indicates a country difficult to travel through primarily because of the rugged terrain and general lack of good water. These White River Badlands have in a sense become the reference locality for geologists and the term has come to mean rugged eroded terrain of remnant surfaces dissected by numerous gullies and arroyos. They occur where the widespread peneplain is being actively dissected by renewed erosion. In this case, the colorfully banded highly dissected landscapes are fossiliferous and constitute one of the most famous Tertiary deposits in North America. The resulting collections of fossil vertebrates are so large that the Oligocene faunas have been considered a standard for world comparison.

Badlands are produced by the balanced combination of geological phenomena. The fantastic topography occurs because of the coincidence of elevation, the type of rainfall, the carving action of streams, and the kind of material on which the streams work. Buttes, canyons, towers, and other grotesque forms are the result of this balance of circumstances. Badlands are basically a type of mature dissection with a finely-textured drainage pattern and steep slopes. These phenomena only occur where the land lies well above its local base level. The material also must be easily erodible or vegetation will stabilize the surface and prevent minute dissection by water. An arid climate is favorable both because it is adverse to the development of vegetative cover and because rain in arid climates tends to come in quick torrential showers with greater eroding action. The geologic material

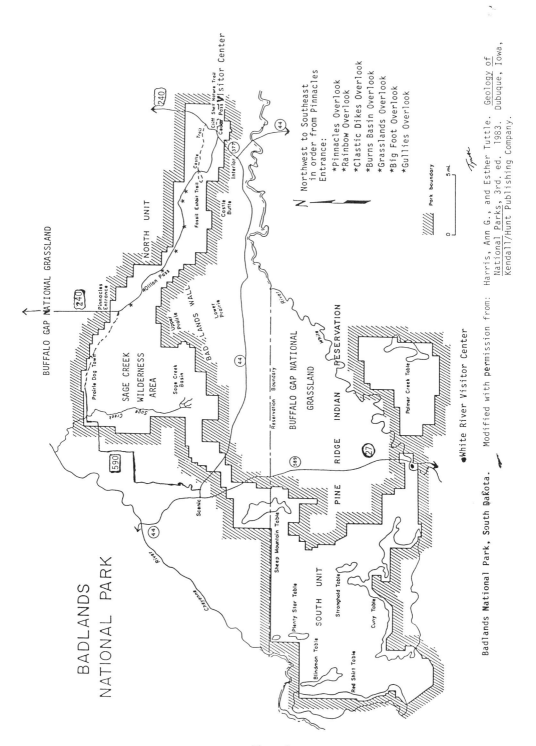

Badlands National Park, South Dakota. Modified with permission from: Harris, Ann G., and Esther Tuttle. Geology of National Parks, 3rd. ed. 1983. Dubuque, Iowa, Kendall/Hunt Publishing Company.

Figure 6

178

of the White River Group consists of very fine clays which are poorly consolidated, with intervals of thin beds of sandstone or isolated concretions. Many of the fantastic features of the Badlands are due to these harder beds and concretions.

West end of Dillon Pass. Photo courtesy of R. Weedon.

NATURAL FEATURES

The Badlands appear to be hills when actually they are remnants. They are in fact a valley and not a ridge. As a result of the Laramide Orogeny, when the Black Hills rose, streams buried the old swamplands with river deltas. As the land continued to rise, and the streams moved faster, their waters eroded the land rather than burying it. So South Dakota came to be divided into prairie and the mountains we call the Black Hills with the obstacle, "the Wall" in between. The Badlands Wall divides the upper grasslands on the north from the lower grasslands on the south in Badlands National Park. Near the Cedar Pass Visitor Center at the east edge of the Park (see Figure 1), the Wall towers up to 150 feet above the upper grasslands and up to 450 feet above the lower grassland areas. During the Pleistocene, for the last million years, the Wall has gradually been moved by erosion northward, away from White River. The Wall is also a water divide.

179

Sage Creek and Bad River drain the upper grasslands, the former flowing northward to the Cheyenne River, the latter northeastward to the Missouri River. The lower grasslands are drained by intermittent streams generally southward into White River. All drainages ultimately flow to the Missouri River, which is to the east. Roads cross the Wall at Cedar Pass, Dillon Pass, Norbeck Pass and Bigfoot Pass.

Towering cliffs of the Wall periodically break loose, forming *slumps*. These disturbed areas have the general dendritic drainage pattern totally split, crushed, and tilted with the formerly horizontal layers dumped on top of each other. The results are holes, pits and even seasonal ponds with moisture retention allowing favorable conditions for the locally lush growth of herbaceous plants, shrubs and trees. One of the largest slumps in the Park is Cliff Shelf. *Faults* with displacement in the colorfully banded horizontal layers are occasionally visible. An example is the Dillon Pass Fault. *Clastic dikes* appear as irregular narrow vertical lines in the Badlands layers. They are basically fissures or cracks which have been filled by material washing or blowing in, most of which is white ash coming from the volcanic ash beds of the upper Brule or lower Sharps Formations, deposited at the end of the Oligocene or early in the Miocene. There are also local deposits of brownish *calcedony* originally formed as

Pinnacles Overlook. Photo courtesy of R. Weedon.

180

a result of ground water precipitating silica on the walls of cracks in the earth's crust. These deposits were utilized as a source of spear points, tools and arrowheads by Native Americans since the time of the PaleoIndians, or PaleoAmericans as I prefer to call them.

Channel erosion has led to *natural bridges* and *arches* which are often quite temporary. The widespread presence of *sod tables* suggests a time of more extensive grasslands in the area. Erosion has left only isolated flat remnants of the once higher plains. The sod in these instances forms a protective cover for the softer soil materials beneath – in effect, sod-protected terraces. There are also places in the Badlands where erosion proceeds at a rate of more than an inch in a year. Certainly an erosional loss averaging at least a half-inch a year would not be unexpected. A century or much less of time can see the spectacular change in the appearance of certain major local features, such as the astonishing changes that have been recorded for Vampire Peak. There are erosional features in the Badlands that are similar to those in Toadstool Park in northwestern Nebraska, where the tops of the *toadstools* are usually composed of channel sandstone, a harder material than the supporting clay pedestal underneath which erodes faster. In both badlands areas there are also many beds of water-worn rocks and gravel. *Mudballs* of clay mixed with pebbles or rocks are sometimes found in dry streambeds. They vary in size from that of an orange to the diameter of a basketball. *Geodes* and calcareous concretions occur in all of the White River Badlands formations, although they are most numerous in the nodular zones of the Brule. Geodes are hollow globular shaped stone units weathering out as discrete nodules. Their outer layer is made of dense calcedony and crystals project from their lining into a central cavity. These crystals are most commonly quartz or calcite, not the same minerals as those of the enclosing rock. When some of the crystals break loose inside, the geodes become known locally as "rattle rocks." *Sand crystals* may occur singly or in a rosette structure from less than an inch to fifteen inches in length.

One of the great homesteader comments about certain parts of the West is the occasional encounter of "water too thick to drink but too thin to plow." Certainly such a comment is very true for the surface waters of the White River country. When streams are running in the Badlands, they are always loaded with sediment. Even when left

181

standing, the water remains cloudy and white in color. Because submicroscopic particles of clay are in colloidal suspension, they carry small amounts of electrical charge that cause them to repel each other, preventing them from settling to the bottom. Pioneers and other early visitors took water strong with alkali from waterholes in the shale and poured it into a barrel of *white water* in order to settle it enough for use. Sliced cactus pads were also thrown into white water, clearing it enough so horses would drink it. Fortunately, the National Park Service now provides good drinking water at its Cedar Pass Visitor Center, for example. Just the same, water remains the main sculpting tool for the ever-changing White River Badlands.

THE MODERN BADLANDS CLIMATE

As with the rest of the Great Plains, the climate of the Badlands of South Dakota is highly variable and frustratingly unpredictable, even more so than the climate of the nearby Black Hills, a drive of just an hour or so to the west. The weather can change *very* rapidly.

Away from most of the major air-polluting influences of man, the air is fresh, invigorating, clean and relatively pure. Humidity is low and winds or breezes are almost a constant. Recorded temperatures have varied from -42° F in January of 1916 to +116° F in July of 1910. Although the days of summer are often hot, summer nights average in the low 60's. Spring and autumn temperatures are often quite pleasant—great times to visit the area.

Precipitation is highly variable but averages 16 inches, most of it as rain during the growing season, as much as 7 inches during May and June. Often rain comes in quick downpours, rushing off the Badlands formations in torrents, sculpturing and carving them. The growing season may average 152 frost-free days, but it has varied from as short as 127 days to as long as 188 days. The last day of freezing in the spring has varied from April 8 to May 31, averaging May 4. The first autumn freeze has been as early as September 6 or as late as October 23, averaging the third day of October. The average amount of winter snow is 24 inches but the region is subject to the potential of impressive but short winter or spring blizzards. Badlands summers are subject to thunderstorms with outstanding lightning displays and probably the best rainbows in the world. The classic postcard photograph of a rainbow in the Badlands was taken by Earl Brockelsby of Rapid City. It is entitled "Pot of Gold." The classic exaggeration for our region of "if you don't like the weather, just wait five minutes" applies nicely to the Badlands country.

A BRIEF REVIEW OF THE BADLANDS BIOTA
Plant Life

While some have referred to the dominating vegetation of the region as mixed-grass prairie, the Grasslands Complex as seen in the Badlands has several aspects. Generally the Northern Great Plains Grassland of the surrounding region appears as a moderately dense short to medium tall grass prairie dominated by Western wheat grass (*Agropyron smithii* Rydb.), green needlegrass (*Stipa viridula* Trin.), blue grama [*Bouteloua gracilis* (H.B.K.) Griffiths] and needle and thread (*Stipa comata* Trin. & Rupr.). Associated species may include fringed sage or the women's sage of the Sioux (*Artemisia frigida* Willd.), prairie junegrass [*Koeleria pyramidata* (Lam.) Beauv.], little bluestem (*Andropogon scoparius* Michx.), silky wormwood or green sagewort (*A. ludoviciana* Nutt.), purple coneflower (*Echinacea angustifolia* DC.), and other forbs mentioned earlier in this volume in the discussion of the Grasslands Complex as it appears in the Black Hills. As with the latter case, there are elements of true short grass prairie, midgrass prairie, and bunch grass types in the Badlands as well. The short grass element, dominated largely by blue grama and buffalo grass [*Buchloë dactyloides* (Nutt.) Engelm.] will form patches with the grassland element described above dominated by Western wheatgrass and green needlegrass, giving the appearance of a mosaic with it. This High Plains short grass element increases in the mosaic during episodes of drought or overgrazing. It also appears as a synusia, a separate and discrete structural and floristic subunit with the taller grass species. The upper grasslands north of the Badlands Wall shows the latter condition, for recent situations have seemed to benefit the grassland. The upland grassland seems to improve in appearance as you travel along the Badlands Loup road northwestward from the Cedar Pass Visitor Center passing by the Big Foot Overlook and Banded Buttes Overlook to the Grasslands Overlook. Things look even better as one goes by the Clastic Dikes Overlook, the Rainbow

Badlands Loop Road northwest of Cedar Pass Visitor Center.
Photo courtesy of R. Weedon.

Overlook, through Dillon Pass, to the Pinnacles Overlook. As travelers look southward and in effect down into the Badlands Wall, there are patches of juniper trees and associated species in the upper partially protected draws or on some slopes. In the South Unit of Badlands National Park at places like Sheep Mountain Table, Cuny Table, or Red Shirt Table, these junipers are also growing on the rims as well, some at least four hundred years old. There are difficulties identifying the species of these trees, either Western red cedar or Rocky Mountain juniper (*Juniperus scopulorum* Sarg.) or Eastern red cedar (*J. virginiana* L.). It appears that at the longitude represented by the Badlands, the local colonies of junipers are actually hybrid swarms of the two species, perhaps surviving from a past time when the species were in sympatry. Their modern ranges are quite allopatric now, the parental species being separated by all of the prairies and plains of central North America. An estimate of the character traits of these hybrid swarms might be 65-70% *J. scopulorum* x 30-35% *J. virginiana* for the plants in the Badlands.

Other than the upper and lower prairies themselves, many square miles of the Badlands clays are almost totally devoid of vegetation. These very sparse areas will have widely scattered individual plants

184

of curly-cup gumweed [*Grindelia squarrosa* (Pursh) Dun.], broom snakeweed [*Gutierrezia sarothrae* (Pursh) Britt. & Rusby], wild buckwheat (*Eriogonum pauciflorum* Pursh), or others (see below). Toward White River there are patches dominated almost totally by inland saltgrass [*Distichlis spicata* (L.) Greene var. *stricta* (Torr.) Beetle]. The Deciduous Complex is found along White River itself, appearing as an open riparian woodland dominated by plains cottonwood (*Populus deltoides* Marsh.), peach-leaved willow (*Salix amygdaloides* Anderss.) and other willow species, box elder (*Acer negundo* L.), green ash (*Fraxinus pennsylvanica* Marsh.), and American elm (*Ulmus americana* L.) where the latter has not been wiped out by Dutch elm disease.

Rare plants of notable interest from the Badlands include Visher's eriogonum or Dakota buckwheat (*Eriogonum visheri* A. Nels.). Uniquely Dakotan, the species is confined to certain badlands in South and North Dakota. It is found as a spring annual on the very unstable easily eroded badlands slopes themselves, living in places where other plants cannot survive. Very distinctive birds help disperse the seeds of Dakota buckwheat, including rock wrens and Say's phoebes, which nest in these Badlands biotic islands. Grassland birds such as lark buntings and horned larks often collect grit on the badlands "pavement," near the homes of a light-colored "badlands race" of least chipmunks (*Eutamias minimus*). Because of the infrequent occurrence of Dakota buckwheat and its endemic confinement to the Badlands, it has been determined to be rare with its habitat considered vulnerable by the Natural Heritage Program of South Dakota.

Most of the few known occurrences of Barr's milkvetch (*Astragalus barrii* Barneby) are in the table and butte country of the Badlands South Unit. Endemic to the west-central Great Plains, the species is restricted to less than a half-dozen known locations in southwestern South Dakota, a few locations in southeastern Montana, and to northeastern Wyoming where it is more abundant. A beautiful caespitose, cushion-forming, plant, it was named for its discoverer, Claude A. Barr, who on his Prairie Gem Ranch southwest of the Badlands, brought a number of plains natives to the point where they could be grown and enjoyed in rock gardens all over the world. His book, *Jewels of the Plains*, was the culmination of his life's work and represents, among other things, hundreds of hours of exploration in the Badlands studying native plants.

185

WILDLIFE

As with other locations on the plains, trappers and hunters killed off most of the game, followed by settlers, so that by the 1920's populations of game animals were much reduced. Since then, as a result of the general decline of the human population in the region, changes in hunting laws and the awareness of people, and management policies of the National Park Service, there has been a significant comeback for wildlife. The Park Service reintroduced bighorn sheep and bison into the Badlands, for example, with the latter doing well. The Audubon bighorn subspecies that was present has become extinct. It has been replaced by managers with the Rocky Mountain bighorn. Grizzly bears were eliminated by the early 1900's, and wolves not long afterward. But mule deer, whitetail deer, the American pronghorn, coyotes, black-tailed prairie dogs, white-tailed jackrabbits, desert cottontails, thirteen-lined ground squirrels, prairie rattlesnakes, bullsnakes, Western painted turtles, and blotched tiger salamanders are species of animals relatively easily located in the Badlands. In addition to the birds mentioned previously, golden eagles, red-tailed, ferruginous and Swainson's hawks, magpies, Western meadowlarks, cliff swallows, turkey vultures, sharp-tailed grouse, great-horned owls, burrowing owls and killdeer may be seen, among many others. Elk remained in the Badlands until 1877, but elk now migrate through the area from time to time. There are even substantial rumors of mountain lions. Bobcats are present, although probably not often seen. Prairie dogs have been managed by governmental agencies over the years because of the potential presence of black-footed ferrets, which frequent prairie dog towns as a residence and a food source. While there have been no recently confirmed sightings in southwestern South Dakota in areas such as the Conata Basin and the Sage Creek Basin where sightings did occur years ago, it certainly is still possible to see one, even though this is one of the most rare animals on endangered species lists. Swift fox, a candidate species at the federal level, is considered threatened in South Dakota. It should be in residence in the Badlands area.

GEOLOGY

Badlands National Park covers an area of some 380 square miles, more than 243,000 acres. The adjacent drainage systems more or less

186

involved constitute an additional area nearly as large. The formation underlying the Badlands region is the *Pierre Shale* of late Cretaceous age, laid down beginning about 80 million years ago. Often black in color, in some places subsequent chemical changes resulted in bright red and yellow colors, as found near Dillon Pass and Sage Creek. Pierre Shale is commonly exposed in the Great Plains. It is marine in origin and its fossils include ammonites (such as baculites), mosasaurs and sea turtles. The *White River Group* is the major portion of interest here. It consists of both the Chadron Formation and the Brule Formation. When the sediments of the White River Group are weathered, they form a slick surface. When eroded and then redeposited, they can form a slick slurry that may be several meters deep.

The *Chadron Formation* is usually a gray claystone perhaps with discrete limestone lenses, a rounded weathering profile locally referred to as "haystack" in nature, and channel sandstones. Formed near the beginning of the Oligocene Epoch of the Cenozoic Era about 35-40 million years ago, the Chadron Formation ranges from 30 to 50 feet in thickness in the Badlands. They say that the Formation is named after the small northwestern Nebraska city which coincidentally is the home of Chadron State College. The rivers in early Oligocene times were rejuvenated, causing them to change from quiet streams to torrents choked with sand and gravel, filling the valleys eroded earlier in the Pierre Shale with deposits. The Chadron Formation is rich in fossils, particularly titantotheres. Thin discontinuous sheets of limestone from an inch to a foot or more in thickness show where the Chadron Formation ends and the Brule begins.

The overlying *Brule Formation* represents the last half of the Oligocene Epoch. It may be up to 460 feet thick but probably averages closer to 330 feet. These are the layers in which the fantastic shapes characteristic of the Badlands are carved, a major portion of the Badlands Wall. An outstanding feature of the Brule is its widespread horizontal color banding, varying from yellow-beige to pinkish-red. This badlands topography is highly dissected, characterized by a series of sharp ridges, gullies, and steep slopes. A rich deposit of fossils includes turtles and oreodonts, the latter in especially great number, even herds, indicating a relatively mild and moist climate highly productive of food for herbivores.

187

Channel sandstones occur as irregular outcrops thoughout the Oligocene layers, so-called because they mark the channels of old streams. Those in the lower section of the Brule Formation are called *Metamynodon channels* because a few fossils of these large aquatic rhinoceros have been found in them. Fossils of three kinds of rhinoceros have been found in the Badlands, one resembling rhinos of today, one light-chested and hornless, and the third kind a heavy short-bodied and hornless animal. The latter, large and semi-aquatic, looking like a modern hippopotamus, was *Metamynodon planifrons,* nearly ten feet long and four and a half feet high at the shoulder. Those channel sandstones in the upper layers of the Brule Formation are called *Protoceras channels* due to the presence of fossils of the horned *Protoceras*. A fantastic-appearing animal about the size of a sheep, it ran and jumped like a modern pig, but the male had a long narrow head with up to five pairs of horns or knobs on its face. Some species at a full run moved speedily like a modern antelope. Layers of volcanic ash are frequently found toward the top of the Oligocene beds, often whitish in color. The ash beds are the most sheer of the vertical cliffs in the higher Badlands buttes.

The lower section of the *Sharps Formation* in the Arikaree Group is represented on the upper part of Sheep Mountain and some other of the highest ridges. While composed of much of the same materials as the lower beds, e.g., floodplain muds, channel sands, gravels, and volcanic ash, these layers are early Miocene in age. The flat-lying mudstones, shales and ash beds are so finely textured, they indicate that they were deposited by sluggish low-gradient streams. These marshy and swampy floodplain areas supported a good growth of vegetation in a climate that was much warmer than now. A wet subtropical forest grew in the area, and the climate was humid. The setting was a broad valley with a surrounding savanna. Monsoonal rains drenched the region and rivers swelled seasonally to carry the sediment-laden runoff from the Black Hills.

A FURTHER BRIEF REVIEW OF THE PALEONTOLOGY

The White River Badlands have been called the world's largest animal graveyard. Remains of more than a hundred species of mammals have been found and are displayed in museums all over the world. An excellent paleontological exhibit representing the Badlands is available in the region at the Geology Museum of the South Dakota School of Mines and Technology in Rapid City. The specimens are so well preserved and of such variety that the fauna have been considered a standard for world comparison. Faunas from each age within the Oligocene are represented in the White River Badlands and the result is one of the best known terrestrial faunas in the world, certainly one of the faunas most often represented in the world's largest museums.

Shells of turtles are the most common fossils found in the Badlands. Other Oligocene reptiles that lived in this lush land of abundant moisture included alligators and lizards. Birds present then included pelicans, gulls, owls, and eagles. The most significant group, though, was the mammals. Most of the modern mammal orders had become established by the Oligocene. The hoofed mammals, the ungulate herbivores, proliferated in the forests, floodplains, and marshes. Carnivores diversified rapidly in response to this proliferation.

Largest of all mammals in the Oligocene were the *titantotheres,* an extinct order of herbivorous perissodactyls, odd-toed ungulates, which attained its peak during this time. *Brontotherium* was a giant example, an animal of twelve feet in height with a pair of hornlike bony protuberances above the snout, nearly the size of an elephant or at least the size of a modern-day rhinoceros. Titantothere fossils are numerous but most are confined to the Chadron Formation.

Oligocene horses were about the same size as a medium-sized dog. *Mesohippus* was an early three-toed forest-dwelling horse. *Miohippus,* its successor, had a large middle toe with two adjacent tiny ones, a trend toward the single hooves of modern horses. Another odd-toed group, the tapirs, were present in the Badlands then. Their descendants migrated to South America during the Pleistocene, where they have survived to the present.

The even-toed ungulates, the artiodactyls, were more successful. In the Oligocene, most of them had four toes. Bones of camels (*Tylopoda* and others) show a range from a four-toed animal of jackrabbit size to a species similar to modern camels. Both camels and horses died out in North America by the end of the Pleistocene, horses being reintroduced into this continent by the Spaniards about 400 years ago. A close relative of the camel, the llama, migrated to

West end of Fossil Exhibit Trail. Photo courtesy of Rick Peterson.

South America early in the Pleistocene. Llamas have been domesticated and some have been returned to North America in recent years.

Piglike *entelodonts,* found in the Badlands, became extinct in the Oligocene. Their appearance was similar to peccaries or wild hogs, but they were not the direct ancestors of domestic pigs. *Dinohyus* and *Elotherium* fossils are possible examples. *Creodonts* were forerunners of the true carnivores, which were more efficient hunters. *Hyaenodon* was an Oligocene carrion-eating creodont about the size of a small bear that was displaced by the true carnivores. Differentiation of the carnivores into doglike and catlike animals took place in the early Oligocene with intermediate forms present in the fossil record for some time thereafter. Most of the dogs were about the size of foxes, but some were about the size of bears, the latter evolving from the dog family in the Miocene. *Daphoenodon* was an Oligocene bear dog. The most impressive members of the Oligocene cat family were the saber-tooths, two species of which have been found in the Badlands, both of them belonging to an ancient group called the stabbing cats. They were larger and slower than most cats.

The golden mole, hedgehogs and shrews were the insectivores of the Oligocene. Other rodents were the ancestors of the modern beaver,

190

rabbits, squirrels and rats. There must have been millions of small rodents then.

The *oreodonts*, primitive ruminants with mountain-shaped molar teeth but unrelated to modern ruminant species, were the most abundant of the fossil mammals represented in the Badlands layers. Cud-chewing, about the size of foxes to five feet in length, they must have roamed the Oligocene plains in large herds. Their skeleton reminds paleontologists of pigs, so some refer to oreodonts as "ruminating pigs." More than twenty kinds then, they have no modern descendants, for they became extinct about three million years ago.

Fossils representing nearly twice as many mammalian families than are known today for all of North America have been found in the Oligocene strata of the White River Badlands, truly a remarkable paleontological story. Great numbers of animals lived in the region then, conditions for fossil preservation were good, and erosion continues to uncover them. We are fortunate that this beautiful, open and free country has such a great value, from the distant and near-distant past onward into the present.

West end of Fossil Trail. Photo courtesy of Rick Peterson.

191

THE LANGE/FERGUSON MAMMOTH
KILL SITE IN THE BADLANDS

The Lange/Ferguson Site provides the first evidence of the association of Clovis hunters with mammoth remains both in the White River Badlands and in our immediate region. Materials from the Site have been C-14 dated at 10,670 $\pm$ 300 years B.P., placing it at the Pleistocene-Holocene boundary, a factor which really enhances the importance of the find. The locality of the mammoth bone discovery and associated faunal remains is about twelve miles north of the town of Oglala and a number of miles south of Badlands National Park. The fossils are embedded in the Scenic Member of the Brule Formation. Les Ferguson, who originally discovered the Site on the Lange Ranch, was looking for Clovis points. The Clovis people must have been very efficient hunters, for they spread rapidly across North America. The Lange/Ferguson Site is also of great interest for the common thought has been that Clovis culture was rapidly transformed 11,000 years ago, as Clovis points were replaced by the smaller more finely made Folsom points often found with bones of an extinct wide-horned bison.

With regard to the mammoths and other megafauna that roamed the Badlands and other places at the end of the Pleistocene, did our hemisphere's first hunters wipe them out or did the hunters' activity along with changes in climate and habitat cause them to disappear? At the Lange/Ferguson Site, it appears that Clovis hunters caught an adult and a juvenile mammoth in a marshy area, where they killed and butchered them. The evidence indicates that the climate then was mesic, not the dry prairie climate now present in the area. The immediate setting was an area of persistent shallow water perhaps of considerable size extending along a valley for some hundreds of meters, bordered by open riparian vegetation of sedges and cool water grasses. All this was found with an open spruce woodland or savanna above the valley on the slopes and uplands. Scattered deciduous trees and shrubs were also present.

Animals in the fossil state found near the mammoth bones included leopard frogs, tiger salamanders, water snakes, passerine birds, several species of shrews, Richardson's ground squirrel (*Spermophilus richardsonii*), Northern pocket gopher (*Thomomys talpoides*), several mice, including the white-footed mouse (*Peromyscus leucopus*), the Northern grasshopper mouse, and the Western jumping mouse (*Zapus princeps*). Other animals included muskrat (*Ondatra zibethicus*),

192

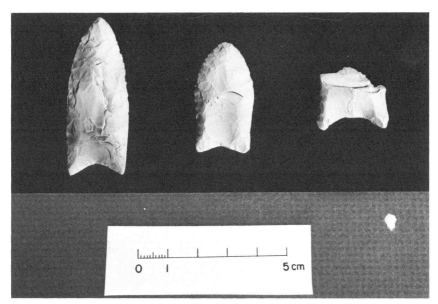

Clovis points from the Lange/Ferguson Site.
Photo courtesy Adrien Hannus.

red-backed vole (*Clethrionomys gapperi*), meadow vole (*Microtus pennsylvanicus*), bison and deer. The modern populations of the red-backed vole in the Black Hills are relict and represent a remnant of a more widespread Quaternary distribution.

The Lange/Ferguson Site is therefore really important not only as an example of a man-mammoth association but also because it indicates the presence of an open spruce savanna or woodland in the Badlands at the end of the last ice age. The death of these mammoths and their burial at the Site were contemporaneous with the end of the Pleistocene climate and vegetation in the Badlands region. These low hills are now semi-arid and sparsely vegetated, quite a different scene in the same location. The landscape now is rugged, highly eroded and dissected, characterized by a number of remnant buttes. Dr. Adrien Hannus, Director of the Archaeology Laboratory of Augustana College, is the principal investigator of the Site.

MAMMOTHS IN THE BLACK HILLS

The Mammoth Site of Hot Springs, a fossil assemblage dated at ca. 26,000 B.P., is located in the Southern Hills in an area where the closed phase of the Rocky Mountain Coniferous Forest Complex (the

193

Black Hills Ponderosa Pine Forest) is the conspicuous plant community of the uplands. The Grasslands Complex is present on the lower slopes and the valleys with the Deciduous Complex being present in streamside locations along Fall River, especially cottonwood, peach-leaved willow and box elder. Located on an old Fall River stream terrace in the Red Valley, a depression eroded in the Spearfish Shale that encircles the Black Hills interior like a "race track," the Mammoth Site now is a local topographic high. The Site is the sedimentary fill of a former sinkhole, having become the top of a small hill by differential erosion. It was on this small hill that mammoth bones were discovered in 1974 during earth moving operations.

Years of excavation later, more than forty *Mammuthus columbi* have been uncovered, of an estimated hundred or more to be found, a mammoth graveyard revealing an unparalleled collection of bones, teeth and ivory tusks. In addition to the largest concentration of mammoth remains in the New World, there are other megafaunal remains that are spectacular. The skeletal elements of the Giant short-faced bear (*Arctodus simus*) dwarf those of the modern grizzly bear, for example. More than five feet tall and nearly ten feet long on all fours, weighing an estimated 1,400 pounds, he must have been a very impressive sight. Other fossil remains discovered so far include the timber wolf (*Canis* cf. *lupus*), coyote (*Canis latrans*), camel (*Camelops* sp.), peccary (*Platygonus* sp.), extinct pronghorn (*Stockoceros* sp.), Eastern American vole (*Scalopus aquaticus*), white-tailed jackrabbit (*Lepus* cf. *townsendii*), cottontail (*Sylvilagus* sp.), Richardson's ground squirrel (*Spermophilus richardsonii*), thirteen-lined ground squirrel (*S. tridecemlineatus*), white-tailed prairie dog (*Cynomys leucurus*), the Northern pocket gopher (*Thomomys* cf. *talpoides*), bushy-tailed woodrat (*Neotoma* cf. *cinerea*), Kangaroo rat, harvest mouse, deer mouse, heather vole, and mink or black-footed ferret. Fish, clam and snail fossils have also been recovered.

For the ten-ton Columbian mammoths and these other species of animals, the sinkhole pond with its warm breccia pipe-driven artesian springs was a death trap. Animals were attracted by both drinking water and the lush riparian vegetation. The big elephants, many as young adults standing 12-14 feet in height at the shoulder, either slipped or ventured into the pool but couldn't get back up the steep and treacherously slippery-wet banks of Spearfish Shale. Many ex-

194

hausted mammoths must have drowned or starved to death, attracting predators and scavengers which were also trapped. Apparently it was an open grave for 300-700 years until the watering hole eventually filled up with mud and sand, the entrapment becoming a tomb.

Palynological evidence indicates that the area around the Mammoth Site was covered primarily with grasses and other herbaceous plants at the time of animal entrapment some 26,000 years ago. Recovered pollen also indicates aquatic plants of a spring and pond environment such as smartweed (*Polygonum* sp.), pondweed (*Potamogeton* sp.), and sedges (*Carex* spp.). The immediate location apparently was treeless but trace amounts of pollen of spruce (*Picea* sp.), pine (*Pinus* sp.), hackberry (*Celtis* sp.), and cedar (*Juniperus* sp.), may indicate wooded uplands much farther northward in the Black Hills. Evidence suggests that a steppe-tundra or Mammoth steppe prevailed in the general area then, with lush grasses, sedges and other herbaceous aquatic and riparian plants present around the rim of the sinkhole. The area must have been more moist and humid than today, perhaps with cooler summer temperatures, but the pond did not totally freeze during the winter.

The Mammoth Site sinkhole area is now housed in a modern visitor center and was designated as a national natural landmark by the U.S. Department of the Interior in 1980. The Mammoth Site is now recognized as a major and internationally acclaimed scientific resource, for it has a unique geological and hydrological origin, it is the largest mammoth-selective trap in North America, and it represents a mammoth death assemblage predating human predation. Excavations continue every summer under the supervision of Dr. Larry D. Agenbroad, Director of the Quaternary Studies Program, Northern Arizona University.

SELECTED BLACK HILLS BIBLIOGRAPHY

GENERAL

Case, Lee (Leland D.) — 1949. LEE'S OFFICIAL GUIDE TO THE BLACK HILLS AND THE BADLANDS. Sturgis, South Dakota. 112 pp.

Casey, Robert J. — 1949. THE BLACK HILLS AND THEIR INCREDIBLE CHARACTERS. Bobbs-Merrill Co., Inc., Indianapolis; New York. 383 pp.

Collins, Charles — 1878. COLLINS' HISTORY AND DIRECTORY OF THE BLACK HILLS. Central City, Dakota Territory. 91 pp.

Curley, Edwin A. — 1877. GUIDE TO THE BLACK HILLS. Rand, McNally and Company, Chicago. 2nd Ed. 136 pp. Reprinted 1973. Dakota Wesleyan Univ. Press, Mitchell, South Dakota.

Dodge, Lt. Col. R. I. — 1876. THE BLACK HILLS. James Miller, Publ., New York. 151 pp. Reprinted 1965. Ross and Haines, Inc., Minneapolis.

Fielder, Mildred — 1964. RAILROADS OF THE BLACK HILLS. Superior Publ. Co., Seattle. 176 pp.

Fielder, Mildred — 1973. HIKING TRAILS IN THE BLACK HILLS. North Plains Press, Aberdeen. 118 pp.

Jenney, W. P. — 1868. REPORT ON THE MINERAL WEALTH, CLIMATE AND RAINFALL, AND NATURAL RESOURCES OF THE BLACK HILLS OF DAKOTA. Exec. Doc., U.S. Senate, 44th Cong., 51:1-71.

Lee, Robert, ed. — 1976. GOLD, GALS, GUNS, GUTS. South Dakota Bicentennial Commission and Deadwood-Lead "76" Centennial Inc. 254 pp.

O'Harra, Cleophas C. — 1913. O'HARRA'S HANDBOOK OF THE BLACK HILLS. Rapid City, South Dakota. 159 pp.

Peattie, Roderick — 1952. THE BLACK HILLS. Vanguard Press, Inc., New York. 320 pp.

Progulske, Donald

1974. YELLOW ORE, YELLOW HAIR AND YELLOW PINE. S.D.S.U. Agri. Extension Service, Brookings, S.D. 169 pp.

Rosen, Rev. Peter

1895. PA-HA-SA-PAH, or THE BLACK HILLS OF SOUTH DAKOTA. Nixon-Jones Printing Co., St. Louis. 645 pp.

Spring, Agnes Wright

1949. THE CHEYENNE AND BLACK HILLS STAGE AND EXPRESS ROUTES. Arthur H. Clark Co., Glendale, CA 418 pp.

Stewart, R. E. and C. A. Thilenius

1964. BLACK HILLS LAKES AND STREAMS. Lake and Stream Classification Report. South Dakota Dept. Game, Fish and Parks, Dingell-Johnson Proj. F-1-R-13, Job Nos. 14 and 15:1-101.

Williams, Albert N.

1952. THE BLACK HILLS. Southern Methodist University Press, Dallas, Texas. 130 pp.

GEOLOGY

Bryson, R. A., D. A. Baerreis and W. W. Wendland

1970. THE CHARACTER OF LATE-GLACIAL AND POST-GLACIAL CLIMATIC CHANGES. Pp. 53-74 in Pleistocene and Recent environments of the Central Great Plains (W. Dort, Jr. and J. K. Jones, Jr., eds.), Univ. of Kansas Press, Lawrence, 433 pp.

Darton, N. H.

1909. GEOLOGY AND WATER RESOURCES IN THE NORTHERN PORTION OF THE BLACK HILLS AND ADJOINING REGIONS IN SOUTH DAKOTA AND WYOMING. Prof. Paper, U.S. Geol. Surv., 65:1-105.

Darton, N. H. and S. Paige

1925. CENTRAL BLACK HILLS FOLIO, SOUTH DAKOTA. Geol. Folio, U.S. Geol. Surv., 219:1-34.

Fenneman, N. M.

1931. PHYSIOGRAPHY OF WESTERN UNITED STATES. McGraw-Hill Book Co., Inc., xiii+534 pp.

Flint, R. F.

1955. PLEISTOCENE GEOLOGY OF

197

	EASTERN SOUTH DAKOTA. Prof. Paper, U.S. Geol. Surv., 262:1-173.
Flint, R. F.	1957. GLACIAL AND PLEISTOCENE GEOLOGY. John Wiley and Sons, Inc., New York, xiii+553 pp.
Graves, H. I.	1899. BLACK HILLS FOREST RESERVE. Ann. Rept. U.S. Geol. Surv. (for 1897-98). 19:67-164.
Gries, J. P. and E. L. Tullis	1955. THE GEOLOGIC HISTORY OF THE BLACK HILLS. *In* North Dakota Geol. Soc. Guidebook, South Dakota Black Hills Field Conf., Bismark, North Dakota. Pp. 31-35.
Hayden, F. V.	1869. GEOLOGICAL REPORT OF THE EXPLORATIONS OF THE YELLOWSTONE AND MISSOURI RIVERS UNDER THE DIRECTION OF CAPT. W. F. RAYNOLDS IN 1859-60. U.S. Gov. Printing Office, Washington.
Newton, Henry and W. P. Jenney	1880. REPORT ON THE GEOLOGY AND RESOURCES OF THE BLACK HILLS OF DAKOTA. U.S. Geography & Geology Survey, Rocky Mtn. Region, U.S. Gov. Printing Office, Washington, D.C. 557 pp., 12 pls., atlas.
Richmond, G. M.	1965. GLACIATION OF THE ROCKY MOUNTAINS. Pp. 217-230 *in* the Quarternary of the United States (H. E. Wright, Jr. and D. G. Frey, eds.), Princeton Univ. Press, vii+922 pp.
Roberts, W. L. and George Rapp, Jr.	1965. MINERALOGY OF THE BLACK HILLS. Bull. #18, S.D.S.M.&T. Rapid City, South Dakota. 268 pp.
Ruhe, R. V.	1970. SOILS, PALEOSOLS, AND ENVIRONMENT. Pp. 35-52 *in* Pleistocene and Recent Environments of the Central Great Plains (W. Dort, Jr. and J. K. Jones, Jr., eds.), Univ. of Kansas Press, Lawrence, 433 pp.
Tullis, E. L.	1951. THE IGNEOUS AND METAMORPHIC GEOLOGY OF THE BLACK HILLS. Pp. 84-85 *in* Guide Book Fifth

198

| | Field Cong., Soc. Vert. Paleo. in Western South Dakota (J. D. Bump, ed.), Mus. Geol., South Dakota School of Mines and Tech., 87 pp. |

Winchell, N. H. — 1875. GEOLOGICAL REPORT. Pp. 21-66 *in* Report of a reconnaissance of the Black Hills of Dakota made in the summer of 1874. (W. Ludlow), Dept. Engineers, U.S. Army, 121 pp.

HISTORY

Cullbertson, T. A. — 1952. JOURNAL OF AN EXPEDITION TO THE MAUVAISES TERRES AND THE UPPER MISSOURI IN 1850. Smithsonian Inst., Bull. Bur. Amer. Ethnol., 147:viii+1-145.

Jackson, D. — 1966. CUSTER'S GOLD: THE UNITED STATES CAVALRY EXPEDITION OF 1874. Yale Univ. Press, New Haven, vi+152 pp.

Kingsbury, George W. and George Martin Smith — 1915. HISTORY OF DAKOTA TERRITORY AND SOUTH DAKOTA, ITS HISTORY AND ITS PEOPLE. S. J. Clark Pub. Co., Chicago, Illinois. 5 Vol.

Krause, Herbert and Gary Olson — 1974. PRELUDE TO GLORY. Brevet Press, Sioux Falls, South Dakota. 279 pp.

Ludlow, W. — 1875. REPORT OF A RECONNAISSANCE OF THE BLACK HILLS OF DAKOTA MADE IN THE SUMMER OF 1874. Dept. Engineers, U.S. Army, 121 pp.

O'Harra, C. C. — 1929. CUSTER'S BLACK HILLS EXPEDITION OF 1874. The Black Hills Engineer, 17:221-286.

Palais, Hyman — 1941. A SURVEY OF EARLY BLACK HILLS HISTORY. The Black Hills Engineer, 27:1 pp. 3-101.

Parker, Watson — 1966. GOLD IN THE BLACK HILLS. Univ. of Oklahoma Press, Norman. 259 pp.

Parker, Watson — 1962. THE EXPLORATION OF THE DAKOTA BLACK HILLS. Unpublished Master's Thesis, University of Oklahoma, Norman.

Robinson, Doane — 1904. HISTORY OF SOUTH DAKOTA. B. F. Bowen & Co., Publishers, Chicago, Illinois. 2 Vol.

Schell, Herbert S. — 1961. HISTORY OF SOUTH DAKOTA. Univ. of Nebraska Press, Lincoln. 424 pp.

South Dakota Guide — 1938. AMERICAN GUIDE SERIES. Federal Writers Project, W.P.A. State of South Dakota.

Tallent, Annie D. — 1899. Reprinted 1974. THE BLACK HILLS, or THE LOST HUNTING GROUND OF THE DAKOTAHS. Brevet Press, Sioux Falls. 563 pp.

Thwaites, Reuben Gold — 1906. MAXIMILIAN, PRINCE OF WIED'S TRAVELS IN THE INTERIOR OF NORTH AMERICA, 1832-1834. The Arthur H. Clark Co., Cleveland. Early Western Travels, 1748-1846, 22:1-393.

Thwaites, Reuben Gold — 1904. ORIGINAL JOURNALS OF LEWIS AND CLARK, 1804-1806. Dodd, Mead & Co., New York. 8 Vol.

Warren, G. K. — 1856. EXPLORATIONS IN THE DAKOTA COUNTRY IN THE YEAR 1855. Exec. Doc., U.S. Senate, 34th Cong., 76: 1-79.

INDIANS

Anderson, John A., H. W. Hamilton, and J. T. Hamilton — 1971. THE SIOUX OF THE ROSEBUD. Univ. of Oklahoma Press, Norman. 320 pp.

Blish, Helen — 1967. A PICTOGRAPHIC HISTORY OF THE OGLALA SIOUX. Univ. of Nebraska Press, Lincoln. 530 pp.

Brackenridge, H. M.   1815. JOURNAL OF A VOYAGE UP THE RIVER MISSOURI. Coale and Maxwell, Baltimore.

Brown, Joseph E.   1953. THE SACRED PIPE. Univ. of Oklahoma Press, Norman. 144 pp.

Denig, Edwin Thompson (edited by John C. Ewers)   1961. FIVE INDIAN TRIBES OF THE UPPER MISSOURI. Univ. of Oklahoma Press, Norman. 217 pp.

Eastman, Charles A.   1937. INDIAN BOYHOOD. Little, Brown & Co., Boston. 289 pp.

Erdoes, Richard   1972. THE SUN DANCE PEOPLE. Alfred A. Knopf, New York. 218 pp.

Feraca, Stephen E.   1963. WAKINYAN: CONTEMPORARY TETON DAKOTA RELIGION. Museum of the Plains Indian, Browning, Montana.

Grinnell, George Bird   1972. THE CHEYENNE INDIANS. 2 Vols. Bison Books, Univ. of Nebraska Press, Lincoln. First Ed. by Yale Univ. Press, New Haven, 1923.

Hassrick, Royal B.   1964. THE SIOUX; LIFE AND CUSTOMS OF A WARRIOR SOCIETY. Univ. of Oklahoma Press, Norman. 337 pp.

Holley, Frances C.   1890. ONCE THEIR HOME; or OUR LEGACY FROM THE DAHKOTAHS. Donohue and Hennebury, Chicago. 419 pp.

Hyde, George E.   1956. A SIOUX CHRONICLE. Univ. of Oklahoma Press, Norman. 334 pp.

Hyde, George E.   1957. RED CLOUD'S FOLK. Univ. of Oklahoma Press, Norman. 331 pp.

Hyde, George E.   1961. SPOTTED TAIL'S FOLK; A HISTORY OF THE BRULE SIOUX. Univ. of Oklahoma Press, Norman. 329 pp.

Lyford, Carrie A.   1954. QUILL AND BEADWORK OF THE WESTERN SIOUX. Bureau of Indian Affairs, Haskell Press, Lawrence, Kansas. 116 pp.

MacGregor, Gordon H.   1948. WARRIORS WITHOUT WEAPONS. Univ. of Chicago Press, Chicago. 228 pp.

201

Mails, Thomas E. 1972. THE MYSTIC WARRIORS OF THE PLAINS. Doubleday and Co., Inc., Garden City, New York. 618 pp.

McLaughlin, James 1910. MY FRIEND THE INDIAN. Houghton Mifflin Company, Boston and New York. 416 pp.

Meyer, Roy W. 1967. HISTORY OF THE SANTEE SIOUX. Univ. of Nebraska Press, Lincoln. 434 pp.

Mooney, James 1965. THE GHOST DANCE RELIGION AND THE SIOUX OUTBREAK OF 1890. Edited and abridged by Anthony F. C. Wallace. Phoenix Books, Univ. of Chicago Press, Chicago. 359 pp.

Neihardt, John G. 1932. BLACK ELK SPEAKS. William Morrow, New York. 280 pp.

Nelson, Bruce 1946. LAND OF THE DACOTAHS. Univ. of Minnesota Press, Minneapolis. 354 pp.

Nurge, Ethel 1970. THE MODERN SIOUX, SOCIAL SYSTEMS AND RESERVATION CULTURES. Univ. of Nebraska Press, Lincoln. 352 pp.

Olson, James C. 1965. RED CLOUD AND THE SIOUX PROBLEM. Univ. of Nebraska Press, Lincoln. 375 pp.

Powell, Peter J. 1969. SWEET MEDICINE: THE CONTINUING ROLE OF THE SACRED ARROWS, THE SUNDANCE AND THE SACRED BUFFALO HAT IN NORTHERN CHEYENNE HISTORY. Univ. of Oklahoma Press, Norman. 935 pp.

Robinson, Doane 1956. A HISTORY OF THE DAKOTA OR SIOUX INDIANS. Ross and Haines, Minneapolis, Minnesota. 523 pp.

Sandoz, Mari 1961. THESE WERE THE SIOUX. Hastings House, NY. 118 pp.

Sandoz, Mari 1969. CHEYENNE AUTUMN. Avon Books, New York. 282 pp.

Standing Bear, Luther 1928. MY PEOPLE THE SIOUX. Houghton Mifflin Co., Boston and New York. 288 pp.

Swanton, John R. — 1953. THE INDIAN TRIBES OF NORTH AMERICA. Smithsonian Inst., Bureau of American Ethnol. Bull. 145. 726 pp.

Terrell, John Upton — 1974. SIOUX TRAIL. McGraw-Hill Book Company, Inc., New York. 213 pp.

Trudeau, Jean Baptiste — 1912. JOURNAL OF JEAN BAPTISTE TRUDEAU AMONG THE ARIKARA INDIANS IN 1795. Edited by Mrs. H. T. Beauregard. Missouri Historical Collections. Vol. IV. 48 pp.

Utley, Robert M. — 1963. THE LAST DAYS OF THE SIOUX NATION. Yale Univ. Press, New Haven. 314 pp.

Vestal, Stanley — 1957. SITTING BULL, CHAMPION OF THE SIOUX. Univ. of Oklahoma Press, Norman. 350 pp.

BIOLOGY

Blair, W. Frank, et. al. — 1957. VERTEBRATES OF THE UNITED STATES. McGraw-Hill Book Co., Inc., New York. 819 pp.

Bull, John and John Faerond, Jr. Visual key by Susan Rayfield — 1977. AUDUBON SOCIETY FIELD GUIDE TO NORTH AMERICAN BIRDS, EASTERN REGION. Alfred A. Knopf, New York.

Buttrick, P. L. — 1914. THE PROBABLE ORIGIN OF THE FORESTS OF THE BLACK HILLS OF SOUTH DAKOTA. Forest Quart., 12: 223-227.

Chase, G. Earl — 1971. THE REPTILES OF PAHA SAPA. Animal Kingdom, 8:20-28.

Dorn, Robert D. — 1977. FLORA OF THE BLACK HILLS. Cheyenne, Wyoming. 377 pp.

Gray, A. — 1880. BOTANY OF THE BLACK HILLS OF DAKOTA. *In* Report of the Geology and the Resources of the Black Hills of South Dakota. U.S.G.P.P., Washington, D.C.

Hayward, H. E. — 1928. STUDIES OF PLANTS IN THE BLACK HILLS OF SOUTH DAKOTA. Bot. Gaz. 85:353-412.

Little, E. L. — 1971. ATLAS OF THE UNITED STATES TREES, Vol. 1, Conifers and Important Hardwoods. USDA Forest Serv. Misc. Publ. 1146.

Long, C. A. — 1965. THE MAMMALS OF WYOMING. Univ. of Kansas Pub., Mus. Nat. Hist., Lawrence, 14:493-758.

McIntosh, A. C. — 1931. A BOTANICAL SURVEY OF THE BLACK HILLS OF SOUTH DAKOTA. Black Hills Eng., 12:159-276.

Over, W. H. — 1932. THE FLORA OF SOUTH DAKOTA. Univ. of South Dakota, Vermillion. 161 pp.

Over, W. H. and E. P. Churchill — 1945. MAMMALS OF SOUTH DAKOTA. Univ. of So. Dakota Press, 59 pp.

Peterson, Charles — 1975. THE TAXONOMIC STATUS, DISTRIBUTION AND FREQUENCY OF THE AMPHIBIANS AND REPTILES OF THE BLACK HILLS OF SOUTH DAKOTA AND WYOMING. M.A. Thesis, Univ. of Illinois, Urbana.

Peterson, Roger Tory — 1934. FIELD GUIDE TO THE BIRDS. Houghton, Mifflin Co., Boston. Riverside Press, Cambridge. 290 pp.

Peterson, Roger Tory — 1941. FIELD GUIDE TO THE WESTERN BIRDS. Houghton, Mifflin Co., Boston. Riverside Press, Cambridge. 240 pp.

Pettingill, O. S., Jr. and N. R. Whitney, Jr. — 1965. BIRDS OF THE BLACK HILLS. Spec. Publ. Cornell Lab., 1:vii+1-139. Ithaca, N.Y.

Robbins, Chandler S., Bertel Brunn and Herbert S. Zim — 1966. BIRDS OF NORTH AMERICA. Golden Press, New York. 340 pp.

Rydberg, P. A. — 1896. FLORA OF THE BLACK HILLS OF SOUTH DAKOTA. Contrib. U.S. Nat. Herb. 3:463-523.

Saunders, D. A. — 1899. FERNS AND FLOWERING

PLANTS OF SOUTH DAKOTA. S. Dak. Agr. Expt. Sta. Bul. 64, 32 pp.

Schmidt, Karl P. and D. D. Davis — 1941. FIELD BOOK OF SNAKES OF THE UNITED STATES AND CANADA. Cornwall Press, Inc., Cornwall, NY, 365 pp.

Strebler, A. M. — 1939. AN ECOLOGICAL STUDY OF THE MAMMALS OF THE BADLANDS AND THE BLACK HILLS OF SOUTH DAKOTA AND WYOMING. Ecology, 20:382-393.

Thilenius, J. F. — 1971. VASCULAR PLANTS OF THE BLACK HILLS OF SOUTH DAKOTA AND ADJACENT WYOMING. USDA Forest Serv. Res. Paper RM-71.

Turner, Ronald W. — 1974. MAMMALS OF THE BLACK HILLS OF SOUTH DAKOTA AND WYOMING. Univ. of Kansas, Mus. of Nat. Hist., Miscellaneous Publ. No. 60, Lawrence.

Udvardy, Miklos D. F. — 1977. AUDUBON SOCIETY FIELD GUIDE TO NORTH AMERICAN BIRDS, WESTERN REGION. Alfred A. Knopf, New York.

Van Bruggen, Theodore — 1976. THE VASCULAR PLANTS OF SOUTH DAKOTA. Iowa State Univ. Press, Ames. 538 pp.

Williams, T. A. — 1895. NATIVE TREES AND SHRUBS. S. Dak. Agr. Expt. Sta. Bul. 43, 22 pp.

Wright, Albert H. and Anna A. Wright — 1949. HANDBOOK OF FROGS AND TOADS OF THE U.S. AND CANADA. Comstock Publishing Co., Ithaca, New York.

BADLANDS

Agenbroad, Larry D. — 1977. *Mammoth Site of Hot Springs, South Dakota.* Published by the Mammoth Site. Caldwell, Idaho, The Caxton Printers, Ltd.

Agenbroad, Larry D., and Robert L. Laury — 1984. Geology, Paleontology, Paleohydrology, and Sedimentology of a Quaternary Mammoth Site, Hot Springs, South Dakota: 1974-1979 Ex-

	cavations. *National Geographic Society Research Reports* 16: 1-32.
Agenbroad, Larry D., and Jim I. Mead	1986. Large Carnivores from Hot Springs Mammoth Site, South Dakota. *National Geographic Research* 2 (4): 508-516.
Barr, Claude A.	1983. *Jewels of the Plains.* Minneapolis, The University of Minnesota Press.
Clark, Champ, *et al.*	1974. *The Badlands.* The American Wilderness Series. New York, Time-Life Books.
Cushman, Ruth Carol, and Stephen R. Jones	1988. *The Shortgrass Prairie.* Boulder, Colorado, Pruett Publishing Company.
Durant, Mary, and Michael Harwood	1988. *This Curious Country, Badlands National Park.* Interior, South Dakota, Badlands Natural History Association.
Hannus, Adrien	1985. The Lange/Ferguson Site—An Event of Clovis Mammoth Butchery with the Associated Bone Technology: The Mammoth and its Track. Ph.D. Dissertation, The University of Utah.
----------------.	1990. The Lange/Ferguson Site: A Case for Mammoth Bone Butchering Tools. Hot Springs, South Dakota, Mammoth Site Symposium. Megafauna and Man: Discovery of America's Heartland (in press).
Harris, Ann G., and Ester Tuttle	1983, 3rd ed. *Geology of National Parks.* Dubuque, Iowa, Kendall/Hunt Publishing Company.
Hauk, Joy Keve	1969. *Badlands, Its Life and Landscape.* Interior, South Dakota, Badlands Natural History Association.
Kirk, Ruth	1983, 2nd ed. *Badlands.* Badlands National Park, South Dakota, Badlands Natural History Association.
Kurtén, Björn	1971. *The Age of Mammals.* New York, Columbia University Press.
Martin, James E.	1987. The White River Badlands of South Dakota. IN: Stanley S. Beus, editor. *Geological Society of America Centennial Field Guide,* Vol. 2, Rocky Mountain Section: 233-236.
Martin, James E.	1987. Paleoenvironment of the Lange/Ferguson Clovis Kill Site in the Badlands of South Dakota. IN: Russell W. Graham, Holmes A. Semken,

206

	Jr., and Mary A. Graham, eds. Late Quaternary Mammalian Biogeography and Environments of the Great Plains and Prairies. *Illinois State Museum Scientific Papers* 22: 314-322.
Nelson, Lisa	1988. *Mammoth Graveyard, A Treasure Trove of Clues to the Past.* Published by the Mammoth Site of Hot Springs and Northern Arizona University. Flagstaff, Arizona, Beautyway.
O'Harra, Cleophas C.	1920. The White River Badlands. *South Dakota School of Mines Department of Geology Bulletin No. 13.*

ADDITIONAL SELECTED READING

Barr, Claude A.	1983. Jewels of the Plains—Wild Flowers of the Great Plains Grasslands and Hills. University of Minnesota Press, Minneapolis, MN. 236 pp.
DeWitt, Ed, J.A. Redden, Anna B. Wilson, David Bush, and John S. Dersch	1986. Mineral Resource Potential and Geology of the Black Hills National Forest, South Dakota and Wyoming. U.S. Geological Survey Bulletin 1580, Government Printing Office, Washington, DC. 135 pp.
Ford, Richard C.	1988. Black Hills stream inventory and classification—fisheries. South Dakota Department of Game, Fish and Parks, Report No. 88-1. IN: Inventory and Classification of Black Hills Streams and Riparian Areas, U.S. Forest Service, Black Hills National Forest, Custer, SD.
Great Plains Flora Association.	1986. Flora of the Great Plains. University Press of Kansas, Lawrence, KS. 1392 pp.
Haldeman, John R.	1980. Non-game bird habitat relationships in the Black Hills National Forest. Unpublished final report to the Black Hills National Forest, Custer, SD. 233 pp.
Harrell, Byron E. (ed.)	1978. The Birds of South Dakota. South Dakota Ornithologists' Union, W.H. Over Museum, Vermillion, SD. 311 pp.
Hoffman, George R. and Robert R. Alexander	1987. Forest vegetation of the Black Hills National Forest of South Dakota and Wyoming: A habitat type classification. USDA Forest Service Research Paper RM-276, Fort Collins, CO. 48 pp.

207

Johnsgard, Paul A.

1979. Birds of the Great Plains. University of Nebraska Press, Lincoln, NE. 539 pp.

Jones, J. Knox Jr., David M. Armstrong, and Jerry R. Choate

1985. Guide to Mammals of the Plains States, University of Nebraska Press, Lincoln, NE. 371 pp.

Marriott, Hollis.

1985. Flora of the northwestern Black Hills, Crook and Weston Counties, Wyoming. M.S. Thesis, University of Wyoming, Laramie, WY.

Parrish, Barry, Michelle Girard, and Ted Schenck

1988. Black Hills riparian habitat inventory. IN: Inventory and Classification of Black Hills Streams and Riparian Areas, U.S. Forest Service, Black Hills National Forest, Custer, SD.

Rahn, Perry H. and J.P. Gries.

1973. Large springs in the Black Hills, South Dakota and Wyoming. South Dakota Geological Survey, Report of Investigations No. 107, Vermillion, SD. 46 pp.

Part VI

APPENDICES

A. DAKOTA INDIAN RESERVATIONS AND POPULATIONS

B. SIOUX RELIGION, CULTURE AND TRADITIONS

Hierarchy of Gods
Sun Dance
Vision quests
Counting of coups
Concept of time
Property ownership
Gift giving
Relationship of chief to the tribe

C. RARE AND ENDANGERED PLANT SPECIES OF THE BLACK HILLS

D. TWENTY SELECTED BUTTERFLY SPECIES IN THE BLACK HILLS

E. LIST OF ELEVATIONS OF SELECTED SITES IN THE BLACK HILLS AREA

F. GEOLOGIC TIMETABLE

APPENDIX A

Dakota Indian Reservations and Populations

There are eight Indian reservations that are located within the confines of the borders of South Dakota: Pine Ridge, Rosebud, Cheyenne River, Sisseton, Yankton, Crow Creek, Lower Brule, and Flandreau. A ninth, Standing Rock reservation, is located partially in South Dakota and partially in North Dakota. Since the headquarters is at Ft. Yates, it is generally considered to be officially a North Dakota reservation.

Summary of Divisions of the Dakota (Sioux) Indians and Present Locations

Teton or "Western" Sioux (speak the Lakota Dialect)

Present Location

Oglala	Pine Ridge Reservation, So. Dak.
Brule	Rosebud Reservation, So. Dak.
	Lower Brule Reservation, So. Dak.
Hunkpapa	Standing Rock Reservation, So. Dak. & No. Dak.
Blackfeet Sioux	Standing Rock Reservation, So. Dak. & No. Dak.
	Cheyenne River Reservation, So. Dak.
Sans Arc	Cheyenne River Reservation, So. Dak.
Miniconjou	Cheyenne River Reservation, So. Dak.
Two Kettles	Cheyenne River Reservation, So. Dak.

Yankton or "Central" Sioux (speak the Nakota Dialect)

Yankton	Yankton Reservation, So. Dak.
Upper Yanktonai	Standing Rock Reservation, So. Dak.
	Devil's Lake Reservation, No. Dak.
Lower Yanktonai	Crow Creek Reservation, So. Dak.
	Ft. Peck Reservation, Montana

Santee or "Eastern" Sioux (speak the Dakota Dialect)

Mdewakantonwon	In Minnesota, Flandreau, So. Dak., Santee, Nebr.
Wahpeton	Devil's Lake, No. Dak., Flandreau, So. Dak., Sisseton, So. Dak.
Wahpekute	Santee, Nebr., Ft. Peck, Montana
Sisseton	Sisseton, So. Dak., Devil's Lake, No. Dak.

There is considerable confusion over the precise boundaries of some of the reservations. When the reservations were established, the entire West River

211

portion of South Dakota was part of the Big Sioux reservation. Then, during the 1870's the government assigned certain sections to the various tribes of the Sioux nation and opened the remainder of the area to non-Indian settlement. The pattern of reservation land ownership is highly variable; frequently as much land is owned by non-Indian as Indian. Some reservations are so completely owned by non-Indians that they have almost disappeared as reservations per se. The Yankton and Sisseton areas are good examples of this type of activity. In addition, much of the land is leased to non-Indians. There are approximately 4,967,250 acres of Indian land in South Dakota.

South Dakota Indian Resident Population, 1997*

Reservations:	1997
Pine Ridge	39,321
Rosebud	19,131
Cheyenne River	8,099
Sisseton	3,946
Standing Rock	8,572
Crow Creek	3,609
Yankton	7,148
Lower Brule	1,263
Flandreau	1,798
Total	92,887

In addition it is estimated that there are approximately 20,000 Indians living in off-reservation communities in South Dakota. The largest numbers live in Rapid City and Sioux Falls. Other cities with significant numbers include Aberdeen, Pierre, Ft. Pierre, Flandreau, Spearfish and Hot Springs.

The percentage of Indians of the total population of South Dakota has shown the following trend:

1940	Indians constituted	3.4%	of total population of So. Dak.
1950	Indians constituted	3.4%	of total population of So. Dak.
1960	Indians constituted	3.7%	of total population of So. Dak.
1970	Indians constituted	6%	of total population of So. Dak.
1977	Approximately	7%	of total population of So. Dak.
1989	Approximately	9%	of total population of So. Dak.
1997	Approximately	13%	of total population of So. Dak.

*Statistical Data obtained from Bureau of Indian Affairs, Aberdeen Area Office, May 1977, July 1999.

APPENDIX B

Sioux Religion, Culture and Traditions

In order to at least partially understand the Sioux, and to properly interpret the reasons for the historical problems between the Indians and whites on the Plains, it is necessary to know something of their religion, cultural patterns, philosophy, general attitudes, and resultant behavior. Ella Deloria in her excellent booklet, *Speaking of Indians*, has summarized Sioux philosophy beautifully. . . . "I can safely say that the ultimate aim of Dakota life, stripped of accessories, was quite simple: One must obey kinship rules; one must be a good relative. No Dakota who has participated in that life will dispute that. In the last analysis every other consideration was secondary—property, personal ambition, glory, good times, life itself. Without that aim and the constant struggle to attain it, the people would no longer be Dakotas in truth. They would no longer even be human. To be a good Dakota, then, was to be humanized, civilized. And to be civilized was to keep the rules imposed by kinship for achieving civility, good manners, and a sense of responsibility toward every individual dealt with. Thus only was it possible to live communally with success; that is to say, with a minimum of friction and a maximum of good will."*

The Sioux people were influenced by religious considerations in all aspects of their existence. Probably the most significant factor in their religion is that man is a minute, but integral, part of a vast universe ruled by a supernatural power that pervades all things. This all-pervasive force is known as Wakan Tanka, the great Mystery, the Chief God, the Great Spirit, the Creator, ... the all in one with no beginning and no ending. In Wakan Tanka, the Great Spirit, all things are one. . . . west, north, east, south, ... sky and earth, ... living and dead. This particular concept of one god endowed with multiple manifestations is not only basic to the religious philosophy of the Sioux, but could easily parallel the same concept in other religions, including Christianity.

In addition to Wakan Tanka, however, there were other gods, in an organizational hierarchy. Hassrick, in *The Sioux* states, "Next in order were the four Superior Gods: Inyan—the Rock, Maka—the Earth, Skan—the Sky and Wi—the Sun. Each has a special area of responsibility in the order of the universe. Inyan was the ancestor of all gods and all things; he also was the advocate of authority and the patron of the arts. Maka, who followed Inyan as the protector of the household, was believed to be the mother of all things. Skan, who was the source of all force and power, sat in judgment on all gods and all spirits; and Wi, though last of the Superior Gods, ranked first among them as the all-powerful Great God, defender of bravery, fortitude, generosity and fidelity."**

*Deloria, Ella. 1944. *Speaking of Indians.* Friendship Press, New York. 163 pp.

**Hassrick, Royal B. 1964. *The Sioux: Life and Customs of a Warrior Society.* University of Oklahoma Press, Norman, Okla. 379 pp.

The hierarchy next included subordinate or associate gods, Gods-kindred, Wanalopi or Gods-like, all being benevolent gods. In addition, there were many evil gods. This Sioux cosmology consisted of a dual concept of good and evil powers controlling the universe long before man arrived. Man was no more than a part of a vast universe shrouded in mystery.

Sioux religion was more than a system of controllers; it was a moral system. It declared that good outweighed evil; it set forth virtues which were to be emulated and penalties for disregarding them. It was also vital. Each member of the tribe was expected to live up to the requirements of his religion. He was expected to observe certain taboos, make the appropriate sacrifices and perform the proper rituals and rites, and be honest and generous to those less fortunate than he. These were simple duties and obligations and it was assumed that he would abide by them. If he failed he was shunned by his neighbors, because each man was in part judge and defender of the common good. There were four basic virtues that all men were expected to strive for: bravery, fortitude, generosity and wisdom.

The highest form of worship of the great Mystery, a profound religious ceremony in Sioux culture, was the Sun Dance. Implicit in this form of worship is the understanding that the sun is wondrous in giving light and providing warmth for the nourishment of living things; the sun is a reflection of the wondrous power and providence of the Great Spirit; the sacred Sun Dance celebrates this wonder. Although many tribes on the Plains participated in various adaptations of the Sun Dance, a particular ritual was generally followed, its central theme being self-torture as a sacrifice to the Great Spirit. It was not sun worship. It was held subject to the call of the "Medicine Chief" at any time, but generally was an annual rite performed during the summer encampment. The total ceremony lasted several days accompanied by many forms of celebration. In addition to the self-torture, the ceremonies combined a large number of prestige-seeking patterns honoring such things as counting coups, vision-quests, gift-giving and virginity. This dance of endurance was an act of divination, a means of ascertaining the feeling of the Great Spirit toward the tribe.

The ceremony involved dancing without food or water for four days, gazing at the sun until the men fainted from exhaustion. Edward Milligan, in his *Sun Dance of the Sioux,* relates that during the fasting three types of songs were sung: "First the song of the buffalo, a song for food, for rains which would bring rich grains to feed the game, speed the growth of the cultivated crops, and would bring good hunting and an abundant harvest. Second, the song of the people, a song for the welfare of the Indian, that they may have good health, long life, and freedom from attacks by the enemy. Third, a song of pleasant days and pleasant nights, a prayer that the weather may be fair so that the dance may proceed without interruption. 'May the snows, the winds, the rains, and all elements be beneficial to the people that they may enjoy more fully life upon this earth.' "

The culmination was the piercing ceremony which usually occurred on the fourth day. "However, the 'blanket of blood' was not an essential part of the ceremony. Some Indians in a burst of thanksgiving or when in grave danger

214

pledged certain things that they would do at the next sun dance thus, one might say, 'at the next sun dance I shall be thonged to the pole by my breast; I shall drag twenty buffalo skulls in the next sun dance; I shall give a hundred pieces of flesh from each arm at the next sun dance; I shall be suspended by the muscles in my shoulders,' or some such vow. Therefore the Sun Dance was the time to redeem this pledge. If anyone had overpledged himself this was the time for charitable people to come forward and take part of the torture. All offerings were based upon this belief; anything one offers belongs to Wakan Tanka, of all things your body is yours alone, therefore an offering involving your body is a true and only offering, thus fasting and torturous dancing are true offerings but to offer your flesh and blood excel all others."*

If piercing was a part of the ceremony, one typical pattern was that the Medicine Chief made two incisions vertically about two inches apart and three or four inches long on each side of the chest of the participant dancer. The strips of flesh were lifted and ends of horsehair ropes passed through and tied to wooden skewers or rawhide thongs. They would attach ropes to the top of a center pole (20 or more feet high) and anchor the other end to the skewers piercing the flesh of their breast. They would dance around the pole and pull against the thongs until they summoned the courage and strength to tear themselves loose. Sometimes the thongs would be anchored to buffalo skulls. It was "good medicine" to tear oneself loose quickly and "bad medicine" to be several days in the effort. Sometimes they offered small pieces of their flesh to the Great Spirit.

The piercing represented the most powerful of all Sun Dance vows. Although self-torture did serve to demonstrate the young man's courage or endurance, the major purpose was obedience to a vow and to give thanks to the Great Spirit for help in battle or illness. A dancer suffered by his own free will to help others and show his selflessness. The dance teaches a series of lessons, according to Milligan: "Bravery because only the brave are willing to enter the dance with its long fast and torturous movements; Fecundity because it shows that through multiplication only can you fully enjoy all of the things of life; Fortitude because it teaches you to pursue your course unswayed by forces of evil; and Charity by the giving of gifts and by taking part of another's burdens."

The young men of the tribe periodically engaged in a customary vision-quest. This was an attempt to seek guidance through a vision from the supernatural powers. It was hoped that these visions would give them the power to accomplish unusual or extraordinary feats. The individual would prepare himself by cleansing in the sweatbath, and confidentially seeking the help of a relative or close friend who would prepare an altar for him in a distant secluded spot. He would then go off by himself to the altar, where through several days of fasting, self-torture and prayer he would seek his vision. Occasionally he would experience a vision which would later be interpreted by a medicine man or some member of the tribe with religious powers.

*Milligan, Edward A. 1969. *Sun Dance of the Sioux*. Bottineau, North Dakota.

215

Among the Sioux leaders, Crazy Horse was perhaps the most widely known for his visionary powers.

Sundance, photo courtesy Thomas Mails.

Sioux warriors also sought personal glory and fame by the "counting of coups". This was attempted during hunting forays or on war parties. To count coups it was necessary to touch an enemy warrior with the hand or a special stick and escape without being struck or injured. This resulted in the very highest honor being paid the warrior. The counting of coups was long remembered and retold at gatherings of the band.

Many misunderstandings between Indian and white have been the result of a lack of awareness or knowledge of traditions, beliefs or even day-to-day patterns of behavior of the other group. It is not possible here to discuss all such causes of problems. However, a few illustrations would perhaps help to interpret why there have been difficulties, both in the past and at the present time. One widely misinterpreted tradition is the Indian concept of time. There is no word in the Sioux language for time as we know it. When it is convenient to do something, that is the time; if not convenient, it isn't done. This single difference in tradition presents real problems for a society such as ours, so dedicated to, and driven by, the clock and calendar. A second difference has to do with the concept of property ownership and security. The Indian could not understand homesteading, barbed-wire fences, or the desire for individual control of material things. Everything belonged to all of nature; the land, the game, the waters, the air. . . . no one owned it and everyone owned it. There was no need for claims, deeds, and

216

such. A corollary to this was the gift-giving and sharing of one's possessions with others. A type of generosity emerged that dumbfounded the whites. If a person wants to give you something, that is a natural and beautiful manner of expressing affection, love or friendship. . . . it must not be refused for fear of embarrassment. The white way is to be polite and decline. . . . this is an insult to the Indians. There are many other simple illustrations that point up problems; they can easily be identified if one wishes to pursue the question.

One major misunderstanding that persists even today, stems from the fact that the white man did not understand the meaning of the relationship of the chief to the tribe. The whites wrongly assumed that one man could speak, and sign treaties, for all Indians. This was, and is, the custom in our form of government. In truth, no single Indian speaks for all others, never has, and probably never will. It simply is not a part of their cultural tradition to govern in this way. The chiefs were always selected within the Tiyospaye and not the tribe or band. They were not governed by the large group, or the tribe, although they served allegiance to it. Thus a particular chief served the people within his particular extended family group and did not represent others. Indeed, chieftainship as the whites persisted in thinking of it, involving a leader who could speak for his followers and direct their actions, probably did not exist among the Sioux before the treaty-making process began, and yet the government insisted that a chief represent the entire tribe.

Another gross misunderstanding, which established a near-permanent barrier to Indian-white relationships, was the whole concept of treaties. Traditionally governments sign treaties with foreign powers, usually following a war. From the very beginning, our government's relationship with the Indians was based on military engagements, or involvements, followed by one negotiated treaty after another. In all cases the Indians were considered as a foreign nation. There was always the barrier of regarding them as foreigners. . . . conquer them. . . . destroy them. . . . there is much doubt that there ever was much consideration given to assimilating them into our culture, and they were to be set apart and maintained on reservations. Treaties were broken or modified by the whites almost as soon as they were finalized with the resultant deep-seated mistrust and credibility problem that still persists today between the Indian and white.

217

APPENDIX C

Rare, Threatened and Endangered Plant Species of the Black Hills

Rare Species

Scientific Name	Common Name	Known Range
Pinus contorta var. latifolia Engelm.	Lodgepole pine	Infrequent in small patches throughout the Hills.
Pinus flexilis James	Limber pine	An isolated stand of trees in the "Cathedral Spires" area south of Harney Peak on the Custer-Pennington County line.
Vaccinium membranaceum Dougl.	Mt. huckleberry	In rich woods of Deadwood Gulch near Lead in Lawrence County.
Viburnum edule (Michx.) Raf.	Squashberry	In rich wooded ravines in the northern Hills.
Chimaphila umbellata (L.) Bart.	Prince's pine Pipsissewa	In rich pine woods at higher elevations.
Arnica rydbergii Greene	Arnica	A subalpine species, at higher altitudes.
Aster sibiricus L.	Siberian aster	In rocky woods of Custer and Lawrence counties.
Helianthemum bicknellii Fern.	Frostweed	On rock outcrops of open woods.
Hieracium albiflorum Hook	White hawkweed	In meadows and open places.
Lechea intermedia Leggett	Pinweed	In open pine woods.
Pedicularis grayii A. Nels	Grays pedicularis	On shaded hillsides.
Polygonum viviparum L.	Alpine bistort	In cool, moist ravines at upper altitudes.
Sagina saginoides (L.) Britt.	Arctic pearlwort	Circumpolar species, in rock crevices at high altitudes.
Saxifraga cernua L.	Saxifrage	In moist rock crevices at higher altitudes.
Linanthus septentrionalis Mason		On dry hillsides.

218

Calamagrostis purpurascens R. Br.	Purple reedgrass	In rocky woods.
Deschampsia caespitosa (L.) Beuv.	Hairgrass	In moist meadows at higher altitudes.
Oryzopsis pungens (Torr.) Hitchc.	Mountain ricegrass	In dry, rocky places.
Phleum alpinum L.	Alpine timothy	In meadows at higher altitudes.
Carex bella Bailey	Sedge	In shaded ravines.
Carex leptalea Wahl.	Sedge	In rich woods and ravines.
Carex microptera Mack.	Smallwing sedge	Infrequent in meadows and on open slopes at higher elevations.
Carex obtusata Lilj.	Sedge	In sandy or rocky openings in woods.
Luzula campestris (L.) DC.	Wood rush	Infrequent in open woods.

This listing of rare species was modified from a list prepared by Dr. Theodore Van Bruggen.

Threatened Species

Scientific Name	Common Name	Known Range
Astragalus barrii Barneby	Barr's astragalus	Dry, calcareous soils, Fall River and Shannon Counties.
Lycopodium obscurum L.	Groundpine	Moist sites above 5000′ elevation, Lawrence, Pennington and Custer Counties.
Listera convallarioides (Sw.) Nutt.	Broad-lipped twayblade	Rare in moist shaded woods.
Adiantum capillus-veneris L.	Venus-hair fern	Moist woods—on rocks, along streams, Fall River County (Cascade Creek).
Gymnocarpium dryopteris (L.)	Oak fern	Rare in rocky crevices of steep, north-facing gorge below Sylvan Lake in Custer County and in deep canyons elsewhere.

219

Scientific Name	Common Name	Known Range
	Endangered Species	
Adoxa moschatellina L.	Moschatel Muskroot	Rare to infrequent in canyons.
Pyrola uniflora L.	One-flowered wintergreen	Rare in deep canyons of rich woods in Lawrence, Pennington Counties.
Gentiana puberulenta Pringle	Downy gentian	Rare in the Black Hills
Epipactis gigantea Dougl.	Helleborine	Near streams in Fall River County.
Polystichum munitum (Kaulf.) Presl.	Christmas fern	Rare in rich woods.

These listings of threatened and endangered species were determined by the South Dakota Endangered Species-Plant Committee.

Nomenclature used is from: Van Bruggen, Theodore. 1976. *The Vascular Plants of South Dakota.* Iowa State University Press, Ames, Iowa.

A more recent listing of rare plants in the Black Hills can be found in: Houtcooper, W.C., D.J. Ode, J.A. Pearson, and G.M. Vandel III. 1985. "Rare Animals and Plants of South Dakota." *The Prairie Naturalist* 17 (3): 143-165. As this book goes to press the U.S. Forest Service is also in the process of developing a "Sensitive Plant" list for Black Hills National Forest.

APPENDIX D

TWENTY SELECTED BUTTERFLY SPECIES IN THE BLACK HILLS

Common Name   Scientific Name

1. Silver-Spotted Skipper   *Epargyreus clarus clarus* (Cramer)

   Largest and best known Black Hills skipper, found in foothill and prairie gulches from late May to early August. Males perch in clearings near woods to await females, adults sip nectar and mud, larvae feed on woody legumes.

2. Say's Parnassian   *Parnassius phoebus sayii* W.H. Edwards

   Locally abundant during June-July in open rocky areas and meadows where the larval food plant, stonecrop, grows. In flight they appear to flutter like some moths, although they are strong and determined fliers.

3. Zelicaon Swallowtail   *Papilio zelicaon* W.H. Edwards ssp.

   Fairly common throughout spring to fall in meadows and forest openings. Males patrol rocky hilltops such as Terry Peak in search of females to mate, caterpillars feed on wild parsley and fennel.

4. Canadian Tiger Swallowtail   *Pterourus glaucus canadensis* (Rothschild and Jorden)

   Most common swallowtail in Black Hills. Males patrol stream courses in search of mates and congregate at mud puddles or wet sand. Larval food plants are various deciduous trees and shrubs.

5. Two-Tailed Swallowtail *Pterourus multicaudatus* (W.F. Kirby)

   Largest swallowtail in Black Hills. Prefers semiarid canyon bottoms. Larval food plants are wild plum, wild cherry and ash.

6. Pine White *Neophasia menapia menapia* (C. and R. Felder)

   Most abundant during late July-September, adults often seen floating with lazy flight about tops of pine trees. Larvae feed on Ponderosa Pine. At times considered a forest pest.

221

7. Johnson's Marble *Euchloe ausonides palaeoreios* K. Johnson

   Fairly common during April to July in moist mountain areas, often among pine and aspen forests. Flies low and erratic, caterpillars feed on mustards.

8. Krauth's Sulfur *Colias alexandra krauthii* Klots

   Restricted to Black Hills, common in June and July. Males congregate at mud puddles/damp earth near streams, roadsides and meadows. Larvae feed on wild pea, locoweed and lupine.

9. Western Banded Elfin *Incisalia eryphon eryphon* (Boisduval)

   Common in spring and early summer, among first butterflies to appear in spring. Large numbers often seen nectaring at gooseberry, overwinter as pupae, larvae feed on young shoots of Ponderosa pine.

10. Valerie's Tailed Blue *Everes amyntula valeriae* Clench

    Local, but common where found, flight May to July. Prefers partially shaded slopes with nearby water, most utilized larval food plant is crazyweed.

11. Greenish Blue *Plebejus saepiolus* (Boisduval) ssp.

    Abundant in open meadows, along streams, and roadsides in June and July. Adult males often seen in large numbers at moist soil, larvae feed on various species of wild clover.

12. Aphrodite *Speyeria aphrodite* (Fabricius) ssp.

    Common in open meadows during July and August. Several may be seen taking nectar at the same thistle flower, larvae feed on violets.

13. Edward's Fritillary *Speyeria edwardsii* (Reakirt)

    Common in open pine forest and grasslands from mid-June to September. Adults nectar at thistles and coneflowers, caterpillars feed on violets.

14. Atlantis Fritillary *Speyeria atlantis* (W.H. Edwards)

    Most abundant member of genus in the Black Hills. Adults may be found from late June to September and prefer wet meadows where they nectar avidly at thistle and mints, larvae feed on violets.

222

15. Pearl Crescent　　　　　*Phyciodes tharos tharos* (Drury)

One of most common butterflies in the Black Hills during June to August. Found in open spaces, meadows, and trails, congregates at mud puddles, larvae feed on asters.

16. Zephur Angelwing　　　*Polygonia zephyrus* (W.H. Edwards)

Fairly common along streams, roads, and trails near forest edge from April to late fall. Undersides of wings resemble tree bark thus providing camouflage for protection from predators, adults overwinter.

17. Milbert's Tortoise Shell　　*Aglais milberti milberti* (Godart)

Common throughout Hills in open areas and meadows from spring to fall. Frequents mud puddles, larvae feeds on stinging nettle, overwinters as adult.

18. Oberfoell's Admiral　　　*Basilarchia weidemyerii oberfoelli*
　　　　　　　　　　　　　　　　　　　(F.M. Brown)

Common along streams, frequently seen perching on bushes or low trees defending its territory. Larvae feed on aspen and willow leaves.

19. Prairie Ringlet　*Coenonympha inornata* W.H. Edwards ssp.

Abundant during early summer in prairies and meadows. Weak and low flight, larvae feed on various grasses.

20. Uhler's Arctic　　　　　　*Oeneis uhleri* (Reakirt) ssp.

Uncommon, mid-June through July, found in open country. Prefers well-drained slopes. When alarmed they may hide in the grass, larvae feed on grass.

Note: This list was prepared by Gary Marrone, Wildlife Division, S.D. Dept. of Game, Fish and Parks.

223

APPENDIX E

List of Elevations of Selected Sites in the Black Hills Area

Cities and Towns

Belle Fourche	3017
Buffalo Gap	3260
Custer	5318
Deadwood	4535
Deerfield	6000
Edgemont	3459
Hermosa	3300
Hill City	4979
Hot Springs	3464
Keystone	4352
Lead	5320
Mystic	4855
Nemo	4624
Newcastle (Wyo.)	4317
Piedmont	3463
Pringle	4879
Rapid City	3140
Rochford	5278
Rockerville	4369
Spearfish	3647
Sturgis	3440
Sundance (Wyo.)	4769
Tilford	3378

Points of Interest

Bear Butte	4422
Bear Mountain	7166
Crooks Tower	7140
Crow's Nest	7048
Custer Peak	6794
Devils Tower (Wyo.)	5117
Harney Peak	7242
Inyan Kara Mountain	6870
Jewel Cave	5090
Mt. Coolidge	6400
Mt. Rushmore	6040
Sheep Mountain (Badlands)	3500
Sylvan Lake	6250
Terry Peak	7071
Wind Cave	4100

APPENDIX F
GEOLOGIC TIME TABLE

ERA	PERIOD	EPOCH		BEGINNING OF INTERVAL (MILLION YEARS)
CENOZOIC	QUATERNARY	Recent		.01
		Pleistocene		1
	TERTIARY	Pliocene		13
		Miocene		25
		Oligocene		36
			UPPER	45
			MIDDLE	52
			LOWER	58
		Eocene		
		Paleocene		63
MESOZOIC	CRETACEOUS	UPPER		72
				84
		———		90
		LOWER		110
				120
				135
	JURASSIC	UPPER		
		MIDDLE		166
		LOWER		181
	TRIASSIC	UPPER		200
		MIDDLE		
		LOWER		(230)
PALEOZOIC	PERMIAN	UPPER		
		MIDDLE		260
		LOWER		280
	CARBONIFEROUS PENNSYLVANIAN			320
	CARBONIFEROUS MISSISSIPPIAN			345
	DEVONIAN	UPPER		(365)
		MIDDLE		390
		LOWER		405
	SILURIAN			(425)
	ORDOVICIAN	UPPER		445
		MIDDLE		
		LOWER		500
	CAMBRIAN	UPPER		530
		MIDDLE		
		LOWER		600
	PRE-CAMBRIAN			

225